Sixty Years in America

Sixty Years in America

Anthropological Essays

Helene E. Hagan

To order additional copies of this book, contact:
Xlibris
1-888-795-4274
www.Xlibris.com
Orders@Xlibris.com
801496

Contents

PREFACE

"In the midst of winter, I found there was within me an invincible summer." (Albert Camus)

I was born in Morocco, a North African country which is regarded as a land of mysticism and erudite spiritual knowledge in the entire Arabic world. Its name, Maghreb, means "the Far West", or "The Land of the Setting Sun" for Arabs of the Middle East. It is a region which has given birth to a considerable number of holy men, visionaries and scholars. The visit of a traveling sage from Morocco is generally believed to bring unusual tidings, and his words are heeded. The land of Morocco is the land of "baraka" - spiritual power - of great abundance. The sacred bird of the country is the Marabou stork. Marabout, and the name of "Marabout" is also given to the various saintly individuals and the shrines and tombs of the miracle workers who have passed away and whose baraka continues to grow beyond their temporal lives. It is important to stress, however, that even though the country is often known as being a Muslim country, it is not essentially Arabic, but numerically and genetically predominantly Berber or Amazigh. Indeed all of North Africa is called "Tamazgha" by indigenous Amazigh peoples of Morocco, Algeria, Tunisia, Libya and the Imazighen Tuareg groups who inhabit the Sahara Desert, south of those countries.

Such was the environment in which I grew up, among Arabs, Berbers, Jews and Europeans of several origins, mainly from France, Spain and Italy. My father was an exiled Catalan who arrived in the early days of the French Protectorate of Morocco, with a few francs and a banjo, and made a living of his talent as a musician and singer in Marrakesh where he first settled in 1925. My mother, whom he met in Rabat a few years later, was a French Jewish Berber from Algeria, whose ancestry can be traced far back in that country, with ties to Spanish and Tunisian Judeo-Berber culture which existed there long before the arrival of France and the colonization that followed. Through my mother, born Levy, I am both a member of The Great Tribe of Levites who were assigned the responsibility of the altar under Mosaic rule, and a member of the Kabyls (The People) who are aboriginals of North Africa, and whose presence in Africa anteceded the invasions of Romans, Turks and Europeans. Amazigh groups of North Africa continue to observe ancient sacred teachings and ceremonies in an official Muslim world. Through my father, I carry the famous independent traits of Catalans and their love of music and dance. Catalonia was also the land of the earliest troubadours who sang of the spiritual aspects of womanhood for the first time in Europe. It is a region still renown for its sunshine, its colorful culture and wry sense of humor.

I was taught in French, Arabic, Latin, Greek and English in an all-girls high school of excellent reputation in Rabat. I studied the Classics, Art History and Philosophy. At age 11, I met a Franciscan missionary brother, Brother Danset, who served as Catechist for our high school, and he introduced me to the Archbishop of Morocco when they selected me for a special ceremony of dedication to Mary Mother of God, on behalf of the Catholic community of the Archdiocese of Rabat, in the Saint Peter's Cathedral of Rabat, the capital of Morocco. The imposing cathedral is still standing today on the well known Al Joulan place which has changed its name, as have the majority of streets and sites following independence in 1956. It was a supremely important event of my adolescence. After a couple of years of university studies in France, I entered the United States as a student in American Civilization, under some special, unique circumstances. Having played a minor role in the relations between the government of the United States and that of Morocco represented by three ministers of the Sultan's Cabinet, in the summer of 1959, the ministers thanked me and offered their help in return for my services: following a phone call on my part, my visa was obtained within hours after the Minister of the Interior requested it from the American Ambassador. The Ambassador was baffled by a diplomatic request he apparently could not refuse, expressed his astonishment repeatedly, and admonished me at length about gratitude and responsibility, and the great privilege just bestowed upon me. I left Morocco two days later for a journey which has lasted a life time. It is my sincere hope that my life and work would do honor to the Ambassador's instructions.

I married and raised three children in California, while pursuing my studies. I obtained my License-es-Lettres from the University of Bordeaux, France, and a graduate degree from Stanford University in French and Education. I owned and managed a Palo Alto boutique importing French swimwear and lingerie, "La Ruche, French Imports" from 1973 to 1978. I then obtained the equivalent to a Bachelor's degree in Psychology and entered a PhD program in Psychology which I quickly left for anthropological studies at Stanford University. It is at that time that American Indians began to enter my life. I was invited to South Dakota where I lived and pursued fieldwork at Yellow Thunder Camp in the Black Hills and at the Oglala Lakota College on Pine Ridge Indian Reservation for some three years. During those years, I created a photo project and obtained a grant from the South Dakota Committee on the Humanities to conduct an oral history project among elders of the reservation. My fieldwork allowed me to establish a number of friendships with Lakota women who welcomed me in their midst, guided me, and provided a substantial network for my work. I attended some ceremonies and was granted many opportunities to discuss historical and spiritual matters with a number of traditional men and women, as well as spiritual leaders of the Oglala Lakota people of Pine Ridge Reservation and other reservations in South Dakota. I owe a great deal to such special moments of friendship, and many kind individuals.

Indeed, I owe much to a variety of teachers who have touched my life and inspired me on a unique life journey, in Morocco, from the markets of Fez to the school benches of Rabat, to thinkers such as Voltaire and Albert Camus whose philosophies have offered important guidelines early in life and nourished my adolescent heart and soul. As an adult, I found inspiration again in the writings of Carl Jung and his disciples. At Stanford University, I learned a new discipline which helped charter the course of my professional years, under the guidance of Anthropology professors Dr. Bill Durham, Dr. James L. Gibbs, Jr., and Dr. George Spindler. Mostly, throughout the years, I have highly valued the caring emotional support of a loving French family, and of my children, Phillip Durk, Jennifer Jane, and Marianne Elizabeth. I dedicate this book to them.

Forest Knolls, California
October 10, 1989

Introduction

In the course of the last 60 years, I have written a good number of essays and stories on topics ranging from memories of my childhood in Morocco (*Mustapha*, Per/Se Magazine, Stanford University Press 1969) to American Indian cultural issues (*Plastic Medicine People*, Sonoma County Democrat Press, 1989) and scholarly articles and reviews of books on Berber or Amazigh culture which have been published in a variety of publications and are in some cases available on the internet.

I have gathered the majority of these essays to compose this book with the hope that it will be a valuable addition to the books I have published earlier, and will indeed complement them. *Sixty Years in America* is not a reprint of its predecessor *Fifty Years in America* published in 2013, but contains most of the same essays.

I have my favorite pieces of course, but each one of the articles included in this compilation derives from a special topic of interest, and some of them are the result of months of research into one particular topic. For instance, *"The Field of Golden Mummies"* (1999) preceded two years of research in Egyptology, the study of hieroglyphs, and the writing of *"The Shining Ones: Etymological Essay on the Amazigh Roots of Ancient Egyptian Civilization"* (2001).

I feel very strongly about the piece which examined a speech falsely attributed to Chief Seattle. I presented the evidence on the actual origin of such a speech on Thanksgiving Day during an American Indian program on KPFA radio station in Berkeley, Ca, hosted by two good friends, Titus Frenchman (Oklahoma Lenape) and Kathy Rosenmeyer (Washington Quinault.) I have completed a fully developed manuscript which I might someday publish on the matter of the lack of authenticity of speeches attributed to Chief Seattle, a Northwestern Suquamish American Indian. The excessive abuse of the words forged by a couple of white men, cited in books, and passing for the wisdom of an American Indian Chief is remarkable and astonishing, to say the least.

My favorite tongue in cheek article, *The People of Niram*, was written on the eve of my departure from Marin County in August 1998, as I relocated to Southern California. I sent it as a letter to the Editor of the Coastal Post newspaper, and it was not until a couple of years later that I realized it had been published by them, as it appeared on the internet with favorable comments on the part of its readers. I am particularly fond of this "Farewell to Marin County" letter I left behind. To this day, it makes me smile when I read it.

The most difficult one to compose was undoubtedly the report on the enslavement of Africans by Arabs, a report which was requested by an international group of Imazighen (Berbers of North Africa and Tuaregs of the Sahara Desert) planning to attend a United Nations gathering in Durban, South Africa, on the topic of discrimination. I was asked if I could gather as much information possible on the role of Berbers in the infamous Trans-Saharan Slave Trade, as it appeared that a large contingent of sub-Saharan representatives were bringing accusations against North African Berbers and Arabs lumped together as culprits of that trade. I was told that other scholars of the group were conducting the same work in French, and I needed to establish facts to the best of my ability and furnish a report in English for the Conference. The goal was not to implicate or exonerate any particular group of people, but to unearth all possible information and reach "the truth" about the role of Berbers. I delved into months of research at the UCLA Library, consulting all I could in both French and English documents on the matter of this slave trade, starting with the writings of Arabic essayists of the Middle Ages on the conquest of North Africa. I have distilled that information in the article I prepared for publication, and listed the sources of the information. It was indeed a difficult assignment, but I learned much important and often neglected history in the process.

My very favorite piece is the one I have titled *"Apuleius of Madaurus: Amazigh Philosopher and World Advocate"* which appeared in "The Amazigh Voice," a scholarly publication of the Amazigh Cultural Association in America. I have been familiar with prior studies of an Apuleius tale "The Golden Ass" through Jungian writings, going back to the 1980's. I knew Marie-Louise Von Franz, a personal assistant to Dr. Carl Jung, who visited Los Angeles in 1980. I respect her enormous contribution to Jungian literature. She, however, analyzed the story from an erroneous perspective, in my view, because she missed a great deal of important data, given the Amazigh (Berber) origin of the story teller, in a study which has become famous among Jungian analysts worldwide. Her failure to recognize Apuleius as a North African man rather than a Roman literary figure led her to falsely analyze the nature of his opus and the meaning of his spiritual journey. Apuleius was, before anything else, an Amazigh personality in a Roman-controlled cultural environment, and his *"Apologia"* which I consulted for this article offered a great deal of feelings about his Amazigh identity. I wrote that article with passion and I hope clarity of mind and expression. It remains my favorite piece of writing.

For this latest compilation of my essays, I have included three important articles which I wrote since the publication of my first book of essays, "Fifty Years in America" in 2013. The first addition is a commentary on the *Amazigh Movement in Morocco* which originally appeared in the cultural section of Amazigh World News, a web site originating from Boston. The second inclusion is a chapter from the book I published in 2018, "Russell Means, The European Ancestry of a Militant Indian", titled *French Indians of America*. As a French scholar living in America, I am particularly proud of the research behind that essay.

Helene Hagan working on photo project with hereditary headman Charlie Under Baggage, in Pine Ridge Indian Reservation, South Dakota 1984. Helene was Director of the Visual Identification Project, Oglala Lakota College Archives, funded by the South Dakota Committee on Humanities (1983-1985). The Photo Exhibit was shown in several National Parks and on recommendation of Senator Daschle of South Dakota, at the Rotunda Building, Washington, D. C.

TIRAILLEURS MAROCAINS

Mustapha

During the Protectorate years of Morocco (1912-1956), the French Civil Service employed legions of men as 'chaouchs', couriers and office helpers. There was none better than Mustapha, my father's helper for nearly thirty years. He had adopted my father in Marrakesh when he arrived in the early years of the Protectorate, young and destitute, carrying a banjo and a few francs. He fed him and lodged him. Later, when my father obtained a post with the French government, he requested Mustapha to be his special courier. When I was born in 1939, Mustapha was already of an advanced age though his age could only be guessed. He was a World War I veteran and took pride in his uniform, royal blue or khaki according to the seasons, which he wore all his life. Three rows of colorful medals and ribbons decorated the left side of his chest, a tribute to his courage and his dedicated service to the French infantry. Below the immaculate turban which wrapped his closely shaven head, his swarthy face had indeed the martial look of an old warrior's, and though his angular frame grew thinner with years, and his features more heavily lined, he never lost his alertness and precision of movements.

A number of my childhood recollections revolve around Mustapha. During World War II, my father was regional Controller for the district of Oujda. We lived in a large villa furnished by the French Government for his office as well as our residence. Our household was composed of several women, one of them a Spanish nanny, and a married couple working in the offices. A number of uncles, aunts, and cousins came and went, some staying for extended periods of time. Mustapha lodged in a little cottage on the property behind the main house and was in charge of us whenever my parents had to absent themselves. Perhaps my earliest memory in life is the silhouette of the burnoosed, hooded Arab by my crib, the same one who would sit at my father's door in the corridor during the day. I grew up to think that indeed Mustapha was a member of my family, as maids came and went, friends of the family did too, and numerous visitors, but Mustapha was my constant companion, and the best story teller I knew. It was from the illiterate old man that I learned the fascinating tales of Islam which delight young and old throughout the market places of Morocco and the Middle East. He also was the first one to put paper and pencil in my hands, and encouraged my early scribbling and drawings.

On warm evenings, my older brother and I would scamper off to the garden near the cottage to curiously watch him tend the carrots and turnips he grew and stewed for the traditional couscous of his meals. Twice a week, we would eagerly await the precious slices of crunchy bread from the round loaves he baked in the domed clay oven he had built in the open. At times, the cleaning women who, earlier during the day, brought their own floured kesras (round bread) to bake while they worked, would gather by the cottage, chatting volubly in fluid Berber while sipping on glasses of hot mint tea. Unforgettable are the serenity and savor of those evenings, when the subtle fragrance of crushed mint leaves and the warm scent of fresh bread intermingled and permeated the air, accompanied by laughter and Berber voices.

When my father was transferred to Fez in 1945, Mustapha moved along with us. Though he no longer lived with us, he would come every day to the gate of my school in the afternoon, and the two of us perched on an old bicycle would ride back to my father's office. Later on in the evening, I would wander among the jasmine and rose perfumes of the gardens which he watered at the end of each work day.

In the evening, Mustapha was busy about our villa. A widower without children, he had adopted us, and we, in turn, knew him as our only grandfather. We went to him in need or grief. We shared our joys with him. On my eighth birthday, he brought me a goat as a pet, which my parents only let me keep for a while as I would assume it must have been difficult for them to add it to the menagerie already kept around the grounds, including chickens, turkeys, and a large rabbit house. To this day, every family member remembers how I tried to teach the stubborn goat to read, pointing with a ruler to a blackboard in the yard, and getting nothing but 'Behehehe" and no A's from the animal.

When Mustapha built and furnished the club house where all the children of the neighborhood would meet in mysterious rituals, he was formally anointed Grand Arbitrator of all disputes, The Caid, who often had to hear vehement parties to small disputes. I was nine, I believe, when I organized an additional girls' club in a different part of the garden. We held our meetings in an old storage room which he cleaned for us.

Schools did not hold classes on Thursdays. Mustapha would occasionally take us to a Tarzan matinee where we feasted on sun-dried watermelon seeds or roasted garbanzo beans. Our greatest joy, however, sprung from the special treat of an afternoon in the "souks". Through our strolls along the stalls of the most famous markets in the Moslem world, the souks of Fez, I acquired and forever retained a genuine appreciation of the Moroccan craftsmanship and a high respect for the artisan.

Mustapha would steer us, our hands nestled in his firm grip, into the bluish light of tortuous alleys, under the grillwork of wooden beams. The burnished brass, the bright hand-woven baskets filled with spices piled next to the delicately carved woods, the glazed colors of the pottery shelves, mesmerized us. We would stop frequently as the old man exchanged greetings with merchants, and though we understood but little of the guttural conversations, the raucous voices always sounded friendly. We never failed to return with gravity the usual "Salaam al ikoum" which welcomed us along the way, the "Peace be with you" of acceptance.

Each visit introduced us to a new trade. In the cool penumbra of the small shops, filled with the pungent odors of tanned skins or dyed wools, among the filigree silverwork or the heavy Berber ornaments, Mustapha always explained the work of agile fingers over the materials or the metals.

In this manner, we sat and watched the satchel-makers, the babouche shoemakers, the pottery craftsmen and the rug weavers, some barely older than we were and almost as adroit as their elders. We would invariably end, weary and content, in the shade of the weeping willow near the seguia (water canal) of the Boujloud Gardens where we loitered over a glass of mint tea and a hot doughnut or "sfenj", as the plaintive melody of a flute ("noria") whined near-by in the old University.

Mustapha retired in 1949 to Oujda after my father was appointed Finance Inspector at the Ministry of Internal Affairs in Rabat. I was ten. In the years that followed, confusion reigned all around us as Moroccans fought for autonomy, and the government of France sent more arms and incompetent deputies to cope with growing discontent on all parts. Violence became our daily regimen in the news, in the streets where emotions ran high, and in all indigenous areas of the land. French and Moroccan blood was shed, and there were moments of bitterness. In the midst of our confusion, for my generation born in Morocco was sometimes of mixed cultural origins (though a French citizen, my mother is Algerian, of Kabyle origin), we grew conscious of the values that Mustapha had instilled in us over patient years, and understood in a way Europeans could not the plight of a proud people, often scorned and exploited by our own countrymen.

We had not seen Mustapha for five years until, one summer evening, he stood at the front entrance of our villa, wearing the old uniform he must have donned again for the trip. He bore in his old weathered hands a gift of home-made cookies together with the hand-cut rough press which had served to shape them; to honor us, it would never be used again for anyone else and was offered along with the pastries. He smiled a toothless grin, erect in spite of his old age, and his cheekbones jutted out of his drawn face. He had come for advice concerning his pension, and he also told us that night that some Algerian fighters were trying to enlist everyone across the border for the Algerian rebellion, and that his life had been threatened.

My father took care of the pension matter. I think Mustapha's long trip by train was not so much for a pension matter as to have a reason to come and visit our family. Unfortunately at that time, our household in Rabat was restricted to immediate family and not the kind of property we had had in the regions of Oujda and Fez. There was no room for Mustapha, though we felt that he was asking for some kind of protection or asylum in his old age. There was a real sadness to that visit. I do not know what happened to him after my father took him to the train the following day. It was as if he had come for a final good-bye.

That evening, as the hour lingered and the breeze from the ocean cooled the late evening, the old man mused over the recent atrocities committed by fanatic elements on both sides, and somehow a comforting note in his presence and his words soothed the heart and psychic wounds caused by what we were all witnessing. We were all helpless victims of political and military strife. Years of common living and common understanding were being denied by guns, tanks, and political ineptitude. To my father, Mustapha was the old man who had taken him as a son, fed him, and protected him as he arrived in Marrakesh a lonely young penniless man, crippled by polio since childhood, with only a banjo and a few songs. To me, he was the living spirit and heart of a time of childhood where in our household Arabs, Berbers, and Jews (our maids were Jewish young women for the most part) lived in harmony, breaking the same bread and sharing the same tea. Those were now memories of a happy childhood forever gone. For Mustapha, the military invasion of the French and the threats of his Algerian brothers made no sense as his reality had been one of three quarters of a century of sharing. For what he had given to my father of service and of course been compensated for was the smallest part of his life. In Moroccan tradition, one who is adopted is just as much part of the family as one of blood relation. My father had been adopted by an Ait Atta Berber man, and had married a Kabyle woman, from a long lineage of Algerian Berbers.

When Mustapha left our home the next day, it was for me as if an entire past had come abruptly to an end. I was fifteen. I remembered that night how as a four-year old child, my first history lesson, which showed some fierce looking red-headed and pink faced man with a horn headdress on the page of the first schoolbook I had, read: "In ancient times, France was called Gaul, and our ancestors were called the Gauls." I came home crying deeply upset and told my parents it was not true, that I did not know any people looking like that, and the nun was trying to lie to me. I cried for the next three days in school, and refused to accept anything the nuns said, telling them they were liars. Not knowing what to do with my rebellion, the nuns asked my parents to withdraw me from the school. At fifteen, I felt the same rage welling again in me. My ancestors were not the Gauls, those savages with pink faces, but the kind swarthy-faced people who had nurtured my childhood were my grand-fathers.

Today, I still remember my childhood in the souks of Fez, the smell of fresh bread and mint tea in our garden of Oujda, and the old turbaned man wrapped in a military blue cape, who watched over my sleep and gave me paper on which to scribble my first attempts at writing..

Rabat, Morocco

Chief Massasoit
Original photo, courtesy of
Diane Berard

TISQUANTUM

The following story is entirely based on facts researched carefully through documents and in cooperation with the Plymouth Rock Museum of Massachusetts. The Museum hosts a bust sculpture of Tisquantum, and an outdoor full-sized stone statue of Massasoit, the headman of the Wampanoag people. The story adheres strictly to the original accounts of Tisquantum's life, travels, meeting with the Pilgrims and acting as mediator between their group and the Wampanoag group or Sowams led by Massasoit who joined the Pilgrims to celebrate their first harvest of corn. As an anthropologist, I have carefully checked the facts, and have adopted a straightforward narrative in plain language, as if telling the story to an audience of young children. This is indeed a story which I hope will be shared between adults and youngsters as they prepare to celebrate Thanksgiving ceremonies in their homes.

On the Eastern shore of the continent of North America, before the coming of Europeans, there was a small village called Patuxet. The families of Patuxet formed one of the bands of the Wampanoag people who lived on the shore of the Atlantic Ocean in an area now called Massachusetts, a word which was borrowed from their language. One day, a British fishing ship came by and the sailors of the ship captured four men of this village. These men were taken back to England as slaves. Among them was Tisquantum, who was later nicknamed "Squanto." While a slave in England, Tisquantum began to learn the language of his British master, Sir Fernandino Gorges, and he told him many stories of his village, of his beautiful homeland and his people. These stories were reported to friends by Sir Gorges who belonged to a group of people searching for peace and freedom of religion. They later led the first group of Pilgrims to travel across the ocean in search of the land described by Tisquantum.

As soon as he could, Tisquantum escaped and returned to America on board a British ship. Unfortunately, soon after his return, he was captured and made a slave again. This time, he was sold to Spanish religious brothers. At the time, most of the Europeans were Christians. Anyone who was not a Christian was considered a heathen, and could not be counted as a human being unless baptized and instructed in the ways of the Christian religion. So the monks baptized Tisquantum.

Tisquantum fled and traveled from Spain to England where he caught another ship on its way to the New World, then called America. The New World was his ancestral home where all his family, friends, and forbearers had lived for thousands of years without slavery or Christian knowledge according to the ancient law of Peace. When he landed on the shore of his ancestors, he found that the village of Patuxet no longer existed.

His family, his relatives, and his friends, the whole village, had been contaminated by smallpox brought by British sailors. Every one of the Patuxet people had died from the disease and Tisquantum was left alone, an orphan without a home or relatives. He walked over to the next village of the Wampanoag people, a place called Sowams, and told his story to the people of Sowams. Their chief, a "noble" or "headman" called Ousemaquin (later called Massasoit which means the highest "Headman" or "King") took him in as an adopted child of the group and ceremonial brother. This was in the year 1620, shortly before the arrival of the first pilgrims to Plymouth.

Early in the spring of 1621, a man from Sowairis who also had been enslaved and learned English paid a first visit to the newly arrived Pilgrims. They had gone through a very cold winter and were in great need of food. A lot of them had died during the first winter they arrived In America and only fifty-five of them were left. They were dying of starvation, destitute and afraid.

The first pilgrims had settled on the very site of the old village Patuxet. The Indian man from Sowams saw that, and on his second visit brought back with him the only survivor from that village, Tisquantum. The pilgrims were surprised that Tisquantum also spoke their language, and Tisquantum told them his story, how he had been made a slave twice, how he had learned English, and how in his absence everyone he loved had died from smallpox.

Because the pilgrims did not know the plants and the roots of this new strange land, Tisquantum began to teach them about edible plants and roots. He taught them how to plant corn, the sustenance of all American Indians for centuries, and how to tap maple trees for syrup. "Squanto" understood the misery of the first pilgrims. He was himself a lonely survivor from a group which had entirely disappeared. He spent the next months teaching the pilgrims the old Indian ways of life, from the planting of corn, (four kernels to a hillock), beans and squash, to fishing and utilizing herring for fertilizing the planted gardens. He taught them also the way of the Law of the Peace which had ruled life on those shores for centuries.

Before the arrival of Europeans, native people of North America, (nowadays called Indians) celebrated the harvest of corn each year with Corn Dances and Thanksgiving Ceremonies. Under the Great Law of the Peace all elements are thanked in gratitude for food and the granting of life. When fall arrived, the Plymouth Colony decided to celebrate in the old Indian way the first abundant crop of corn which would feed them through the winter with a special feast accompanied by music and dancing. The pilgrims asked Tisquantum to fetch some of his Wampanoag friends to join in the celebration. Tisquantum went to Sowams and came back in the company of ninety friends, to the great surprise of the pilgrims. They had abundant food prepared but did not expect such a large company.

The Wampanoag Chief, Massasoit, sent some of his men to hunt, and they came back with five deer to provide meat for everyone. The first Thanksgiving Feast was celebrated in late October 1621, assembling fifty-five pilgrims and ninety Wampanoag Indians. The Feast lasted three days. In addition to the deer meat, there was abundant food, ducks and geese, lobster, eel pies, corn bread and pop-corn balls, a favorite food of the Wampanoag Indians who combined popped corn with maple syrup they taught pilgrims to gather from the maple trees. Berries and wild plums were also shared.

Thanksgiving was not celebrated the next year because the pilgrims were not able to grow corn so well on their own. In 1623, the feast was held in July in thanksgiving for the rain. Afterwards, for years, people celebrated their thanks for food and plenty whenever they chose to do so, and it was not until 1864 that it was declared an official national holiday by President Lincoln.

In Canada, Thanksgiving is still celebrated on the second Monday of October, as it was originally done. This is one of the many customs modem America owes to the teachings of the American Indians. In teaching the first Pilgrims, Tisquantum put aside his own grief and loss to help other human beings in distress, even though they belonged to the very group of people who had enslaved him twice and brought the disease which killed all his family. Tisquantum displayed a generosity of heart and character which truly makes him a fine representative of his people and their legacy to the history and cultural heritage of the American people. He and his role in Thanksgiving should be remembered on this most *American* of Holidays.

Tisquantum died of small pox in 1622.

CHIEF SEATTLE'S LEGACY

Fable and Truth

Wise must be the scholar who can answer the profound questioning and spiritual insight of this address, or interpret its matchless climax.... The solemn occasion and strength of this speech well makes it the Funeral Oration of the Great Indian Race.

John M. Rich - *Chief Seattle's Unanswered Challenge* (1932)

Such is the Preface of the original address which has become a New Age prayer invoked in books, artwork, and recently in an award- winning 1992 Canadian film, The War Against Indians. There is nothing obscure about its original intent: it was meant to be a white man's nostalgic elegy mourning the passing of the Indians. Chief Seattle (Sealth) continues to be quoted in numerous publications, as if he really was the author of the words attributed to him. However, the often quoted Chief Seattle's Speech was not made by Chief Seattle.

The earliest version of this alleged famous speech appeared on October 29, 1887, in a *"Letter to the Seattle Sunday Star."* This letter was supposedly submitted by a certain Dr. Henry A. Smith, reporting the speech as if it had been spoken by Chief Seattle at the occasion of the Treaty Council of Point Elliott under which the Duwamish Headman signed away his people's territory. The Treaty was signed in January 1855. The European doctor submitted his letter twenty- two years later, in 1887.

There is no evidence as to its authenticity. The few words that Chief Seattle pronounced during this "solemn" occasion are on record. They were not the words submitted by Dr. Smith to the Seattle newspaper in 1887, or the speech quoted today.

The second published version of this alleged famous speech was published in a small pamphlet by John M. Rich (Pigott-Washington, 1932). It resurrected the first text of 1887 with an additional reflection on the meaning of death and the changing world, which is John Rich's own contribution to folk literature.

The present day versions under circulation in various forms are a mixture of recently composed lyrical phrases, interspersed with paragraphs dating to the 1932 version of John M. Rich, all of which have been invented by white popular imagination. The challenge set by John M. Rich cannot be answered in the terms formulated by John M. Rich. One might wonder at the exaggerated and pompous introduction. This challenge totally dissolves when one understands that it is no more than a white man's fable based on a nostalgic view of the Noble Savage. The speech, sometimes presented as a letter, as in Joseph Campbell's and Bill Moyers *The Power of Myth*, is a fraud.

The record is unambiguous. The two documented speeches of Chief Seattle do not include any philosophical pronouncements or prophetic message. He first said:

"I look upon you as my Father. I and the rest regard you as such. All of the Indians have the same good feeling toward you and will send it on paper to the Great Father. All of the men, old men, women, and children rejoice that he has sent you to take care of them. My mind is like yours. I don't want to say more. My heart is very good toward Dr. Maynard. I want always to get medicine from him."

This speech was officially recorded at the Point Elliott Treaty on January 22, 1855. On January 23, *1855*, at the conclusion of the proceedings, Chief Seattle again spoke in the following words:

"Now by this we make friends and put away all bad feelings, if we ever had any. We are the friends of the Americans. All of the Indians are of the same mind. We look upon you as our Father. We will never change our minds, but since you have been to see us, we will always be the same. Now, now, do you send this paper." *(NARS Microfilm Publications 1495, roll 5, Treaties, 1801-1869, National Archives)*

These are the *only* words known to have been spoken by Chief Seattle at Point Elliott and preserved in an official record. A search of the records of the Bureau of Indian Affairs, of the Office of the Secretary of the Interior in the National Archives, and of the presidential papers of Franklin Pierce in the Library of Congress furnish no other information or documentation backing the 1887 Letter written by Dr. Smith. The National Archives and the National Anthropological Archives are two different institutions. The following is a statement prepared at the National Archives and Records Administration and distributed by the National Anthropological Archives for the information of its users, and it reads in part:

"We have received many inquiries about a speech said to have been delivered by Chief Seattle (or Sealth) of the Duwamish tribe of Indians to Isaac I. Stevens, Governor of Washington Territory, during the Treaty Council of Point Elliott (December, 1854—January, 1855). Many printed versions of this purported speech are extant, often with considerable variation in language. The first publication of "Seattle's speech" apparently appeared in the Seattle's *Sunday Star of* October 29, 1887, as part of a letter by Dr. Henry A. Smith. Dr. Smith claimed to have made notes during Seattle's talk in the Duwamish language at Point Elliott in 1855; however, no verifiable version, in Duwamish or English, exists.

In view of the fact that the tone and concepts are so at variance with those expressed in speeches known to have been delivered by Seattle on January 22 and 23, 1855, which can be found among records in our custody, we have concluded that the speech about which you inquired is probably spurious."

The words of Chief Seattle are also said to be contained in a letter supposedly written in 1855 to President Franklin Pierce. That letter has not been found despite many attempts to locate it and must also be regarded as "spurious." The known facts can therefore be summarized as follows:

- There is an entire absence of contemporary data regarding the existence of an elaborate speech during the Treaty of Point Elliott.
- There is no Duwamish text of any such speech.
- There is a total absence of notes taken by Dr. Henry A. Smith on such a speech, which he would have had to record either in Duwamish or English at the time it was spoken or translated. He was not the official translator at the Treaty talks. Dr. Smith

was not placed at the site of the Treaty either by official record or human recollection of eye witnesses interviewed later.

- There is a total silence on the part of all the people who attended the Point Elliott Treaty Council, and meetings between Seattle and Governor Stevens, concerning such a speech before and after the 1887 publication of Dr. Smith's letter. Such a lengthy and unusual piece of oratory would most certainly have been noticed and remembered by eye witnesses. None of them did, even when questioned about it.

- There is a total absence of such a speech in the official record of the Treaty proceedings, while there is a clear record of two actual statements made by Chief Seattle during that occasion, which have nothing in common with the Dr. Smith's version or what was attributed to him later.

- The only two speeches of record are reproduced in their entirety above, and their style and tone do not approach those of the alleged famous "speech," as noted by the National Archives staff. There are glaring contradictions in the statements of Dr. Henry A. Smith about the site and date of his speech and the statement of John M. Rich. The latter had no basis whatsoever, in any historical or private record, for dating it back to December, 1854. John M. Rich introduces his alleged transcription of the original Smith letter with the following words: "In the *Seattle Sunday Star* of October 29, 1887, appeared the following from the pen of Dr. Henry A. Smith:

'When Governor Stevens first arrived in Seattle and told the natives that he had been appointed Commissioner of Indian Affairs for Washington Territory, they gave him a demonstrative reception in front of Dr. Maynard's office near the waterfront on Main Street.... The Governor was then introduced by Dr. Maynard to the native multitude.... When he sat down, Chief Seattle arose with all the dignity of a senator who carries the responsibility of a great nation upon his shoulders. Placing one hand upon the Governor's head, and slowly pointing heavenward with the index finger of the other, he commenced his memorable address in solemn and impressive tone....' The scene is composed and the language is very ornate and dramatic. Its tone is identical in the speech itself, the introduction and the following conclusion. This leads a careful reader to certainty as to their common authorship.

John M. Rich contended that he was told of this speech by a certain Clark B. Beknap who himself was told by a Vivian M. Carkeek on her deathbed that she had heard Dr. Henry A. Smith himself on his deathbed affirm the authenticity of the Seattle's speech. The pamphlet published by John Rich (Pigott- Washington, 1932) entitled *Chief Seattle's Unanswered Challenge* contains no reference to any document corroborating its origin. Dr. Henry A. Smith left no information concerning this speech in his legacy. Today, the paternalistic perspective which gave rise to the offensive words placed on the lips of this Duwamish Indian is no longer in fashion. The tone of the earlier address reflects the viewpoint of a bygone era and all its prejudices. The language of later versions attempted to rewrite the offensive passages and to insert new poetic phrases which unfortunately did not take into account the context in which Chief Seattle would have been speaking. The references to the buffalo and such words as "sachem," to name but two of several glaring errors, reveal the later additions as European folk literature.

The writer of this fancy composition underscores the fatality of the demise of the Indians as a "natural and just" occurrence. "The offer may be wise," the Indian Headman is made to say, "We are no longer in need of a great country.... We may have been somewhat to blame." .....He allegedly utters such unbelievable words as: "The noble braves, fond mothers, glad, happy- hearted maidens, and even the little children, who lived and rejoiced here for a brief season, and whose very names are now forgotten, still love these somber solitudes and their deep fastnesses which at eventide grow shadowy with the presence of dusty spirits."

Such language reflects a 19th century romantic view. It belongs to a distinct genre: that of mourning elegies. Anyone acquainted with the literature of English Lake Poets and European Romanticism, and the work of Edgar A. Poe, can recognize its European tone.

What Indian leader would, in his own language, in front of his own people (since it has been established that Chief Seattle spoke only Duwamish), speak of his own young warriors as "angry at some real or imaginary wrong," disfiguring their faces with black paint, "cruel and relentless and know no bounds, and our old men are unable to restrain them?" Such portrayal of Indian warriors and of their relationship to elders can only emanate from European fantasy. It is a caricature. My feeling is that a whole philosophy was couched in this romantic elegy, dressed in a flowery language unlike any other Indian oratory: underneath the soulful epithets, one perceives the familiar doctrine of Manifest Destiny.

The statement which reads: "Your religion was written in tablets of stone by the iron finger of an angry God, lest you might forget it. The Red Man would never comprehend and remember it. Our religion is the traditions of our ancestors—the dreams of our old men given to them in the solemn hours of night by The Great Spirit and the visions of our sachems, and is written in the hearts of our people," contains a serious error. The word "sachem" is an Algonquin word which could never have referred to the beliefs of Northwest people. The nineteenth century popular use of this word among white men had so vulgarized it that it found its way into the text. Such a slip could be overlooked by a white man of the twentieth century eager to sound "Indian," but was certainly not made by a Duwamish Leader.

The justification of white men's acts toward Native populations appears in such a statement: "We will dwell apart in peace, for the words of the Great White Chief seem to be the voice of Nature speaking to my people out of the thick darkness." It was a time of Indian extermination and denial. It was a time when such acts of genocide were made to look "just" and "natural." A final blow to West Coast Indian cultures was attempted in 1884 with the passing of Bill 87 by the American government. Bill 87 abolished the traditional Potlatch which was at the core of all social, economic, spiritual, and artistic life in these Indian societies. A series of epidemics, the last one occurring in 1862, reduced the Indian population of that area by over one-third. The publication of a so-called Seattle speech in a white newspaper in 1887 went hand in hand with the ongoing slaughter perpetrated in government policies by Bill 87.

The final image of this composed elegy is particularly telling. At the end of this alleged speech, the Duwamish Chief is represented as an old, genteel, graceful, and earnest man declaiming the demise of all Indians in a scene reminiscent of a nineteenth century romantic dirge, and the gloom of cemeteries. The final paragraph reads: "The above is but a fragment of Chief Seattle's speech, and lacks all the charm lent by the grace and earnestness of the sable old orator and the occasion." The word "sable" is extremely revealing. As a noun, "sable" is an archaic word of heraldry language depicting a funerary garment or mourning clothes. As an adjective, it has been used to describe darkness in the sense of sinister.

In this final stroke of black, a symbolic portrait of a dark mourner at a funeral is framed.

All contemporary versions have followed the early model. The speech has consistently been used to illustrate a certain perspective and to sustain a social or ideological premise. The speech has all along reflected the fantasy of the American people about Indians. It is the reason for its popularity, as it reaches to the depths of the collective national psyche. Environmentalists have mourned the passing of the buffalo, a species Chief Seattle probably never saw, and lamented over the growth of urban settlements and couched current concerns with pollution. In the Joseph Campbell's version, it was the need to illustrate his theory of myth. The text has been refashioned each time to justify some feeling which is given the stamp of approval by the defunct Chief.

A comparison between the varying texts demonstrates a magical use of words to say just about anything through the fabricated speech, as if it were an Indian legacy. An overall pattern remains through all these transformations of the text: the writers consistently lament the passing away of a given order of things and embroider upon the nostalgia for its disappearance. The common theme, worked and reworked according to each generation, is nostalgia for a bygone past—a romantic theme.

In the Joseph Campbell version as narrated in *The Power of Myth*, and in a subsequent play by one of his students and disciples, *Save The Whales (1991)*, the speech is used to create a myth of heroic western adventure. The myth of the frontier engages today in verticality, when it was once horizontal. The frontier myth has become the conquest of space.

The association of animals and Indians in a renewed sacred brotherhood, taken up by Campbell, is embellished by his disciple who presents Joseph Campbell as the hero of dead Indians reincarnated in whales. He is lifted into space in a pod on the immortal words of Chief Seattle. Joseph Campbell, reciting the words of Chief Seattle to all the Indian nations assembled in the sea, has finally become the ultimate hero of his own Indians. This reversal is somewhat phenomenal but can be seen as a logical development if one considers that the speech was a white man's speech from the start. The juxtaposition of all these spurious texts, from 1887 to 1991 demonstrates the nature of unconscious patterns across time. The author of the 1991 fictive scenario dramatizes this mythology in formation quite clearly, displaying its goal without obfuscation. The speech leaves the earth in the body of Joseph Campbell, the only spokesperson now recognized by all Indian nations. The goal is universal "salvation."

In Joseph Campbell's view of myth, and in this latest 1991 script, the European fantasy images the American Indian in association with the animal world. Their earlier silence, seen as an inability to speak for themselves, and their surrender of the word to the white man, are turned into the ultimate glory and apotheosis of a white Chief, Joseph Campbell. The fraud is unveiled now, despite all the good intentions of the white authors of this monumental fable to render homage to Indians. It is as if the future had met the past full circle. I found it curious that this latest piece of imaginary "Indianism" fell into my hands unexpectedly as I was writing a book on Chief Seattle's Speech.

Contemporary scholars such as Renato Rosaldo (Stanford University, 1991) have looked at such a phenomenon in a new light. The notion of "Imperialist Nostalgia" is emerging as a field of study among third world sociologists and anthropologists. The theme of "Imperialist Nostalgia" is embedded in western history, and is part and parcel of a history of genocide, Professor Rosaldo emphasizes.

Imperialist nostalgia consists of three movements. First occurs the obliteration of a group of people and the acquisition of their territory. Second, this is justified on the grounds that it is "moral" for a superior group of people to exterminate another which is linked to the realm of nature and animal life and thereby reduced to less than humanity. What is not human can be more easily destroyed as less valuable in the western myth of superiority over animals. Third, the very nature of this act is psychologically denied. The perpetrators reduce other human beings to slavery or deem them soulless objects with no other existence than in their fantasies; lose in the process the ground of their own related humanity; then search desperately to regain it by the intense idealization of nature and aboriginal people, nostalgia for a "return to the source." The composite nature of this phenomenon in three movements is manifest at the core of Western History and constitutes what is now perceived as a persistent sense of nostalgia, a mythology peculiar to the mentality of western nations.

The respect we owe a man is to preserve his true words. When we are falsifying the image of an Indian Headman by making him philosophize in borrowed words, we are defacing his true being. Chief Seattle did not leave many words on record. We can certainly honor his memory by respecting those few words, and refrain from further falsification. The embellishment of his image and his speech may come from a good intention, but it does not add one iota to the truth of the human record.

Originally published in *Journal of Archetypal Ethnology* © 1991

Plastic Medicine People

Originally published in Press Democrat newspaper, Sonoma County Press, California, 1990.

Several individuals have recently brought to my attention that the phenomenon of new-shamanism, also styling itself as "core shamanism", is taking ample proportions in Northern California. I have researched the particular group led by Sedonia Cahill and Bird Brother, known as THE GREAT ROUND organization. This group was targeted as it is typical of this New Age phenomenon, both in its practices and its public assertions as innovator and creator of ritual while proffering a public denial of its Native American character.

There are other groups advertising seminars, sweat lodges and vision quests as if they were indeed purveying true Indian teachings. All such groups follow the patterns followed by The Great Round in as much as they are imitators of Indian ways and are led by individuals who do not have any inside knowledge of American Indian spirituality.

The Great Round teachings

These teachings are put forth in advertisement, brochures, flyers and newsletters in Native American terminology and symbols, as an invitation to a meaningful journey, Indian style. What indeed attracts followers is the opportunity to practice Indian ways, and the people who respond to this promotional material are not versed enough in Native American traditions to be able to tell the difference between the imitation and the real thing.

This phenomenon is prevalent in many parts of the nation, and is not restricted to the practices of Sedonia Cahill, Bird Brother and the Great Round. Indeed these two individuals and their group are just another group in a phenomenon which began with Sun Bear. Sun Bear isolated himself from his own community by "selling out" bits and pieces of Indian spiritual knowledge. He established the "Bear Tribe", composed of non - Indian followers.

Another individual who continues to hold influence in these circles is Hyemeyohsts Storm. This man stands in the background of the Deer Tribe, publicly headed by Harley Swift Deer Reagan. He carries the title of "General Storm." The Deer Tribe is composed of women's earth lodges and men's Métis Brotherhood lodges. For many years a number of Native American leaders have stated that Mr. Reagan is a Caucasian man who has adopted a false Indian identity, as have many of the people listed as venerable teachers by Sedonia Cahill, Bird Brother and The Great Round in their publications.

What makes these groups appear to be Native American, without being Indian or having proper Native American training and teachings, is the use of ceremonial pipes, smudging, the use of Indian names, the making of Indian paraphernalia such as "prayer arrows," tobacco ties, the use of feathers, the use of cornmeal and tobacco in offerings, the use of braided sweet grass for blessings, the making of "medicine bundles", eagle feathers, the ceremonial use of medicine wheels with the four directions, Indian chanting to drums, the practice of purification in sweat lodges and the vision quest. All these practices are the public outward aspects of North American Indian religions, and are well known to be so.

There is, however, a vast difference between the manipulation of objects, or the imitation of rituals on instructions gathered from readings and public knowledge, and the profound wisdom of spiritual practices of Native American people, still in the keeping of true medicine people who are unknown to the general non-Indian population of this network. People who are truly knowledgeable are the traditional elders of Indian nations, practitioners of various medicines, and a few anthropologists, writers, artists and people who have been invited to share in real ceremonies and do not write about, sell or divulge their experience.

The most common features of all these individuals Indians call "plastic medicine people" is the marketing of their limited knowledge, the offering of paying workshops, and the business aspect of their spirituality. All peddle the scant information they have gathered from a few discredited figures or textbooks which have a poor reputation both in Indian country and among anthropologists. This is evident in the reading list in the Deer Tribe Apprentice Manual and the Sedonia Cahill reading list for vision quests. The most common clichés all these people adopt are several statements: they have access to real Native American traditions; Indians do not have a monopoly on these traditions; they have been properly trained by qualified Indian Medicine people; and what they are doing has validity, meaning, and cannot be contested.

They even trivialize the concerns of Native American elders, which they lately seem to reduce to such issues as "ownership of spirit," or "jealousy." Such trivialization and such distortion of the real central issues are not to be taken lightly. They hide cultural projections and indefensible acts of desecration.

The Ceremonial Pipe

Though Native Americans of this continent used several forms of personal, social and ceremonial pipes, the teachings of the Sacred Pipe through The Buffalo Calf Woman came to the Lakota people alone (circa 900 A.D.). This is a real event and not a myth, for it occurred in historical time, as a supernatural event recorded in Lakota sacred texts. It is indeed far more recent than the times of Jesus and the writing of the New Testament, or than the revelation of the Koran to Mohammed.

The Lakota are The Keepers of The Sacred Pipe, as the Cheyenne are The Keepers of The Sacred Arrows. No group has the right to usurp such functions, or to imitate specific ceremonies in any form or fashion without showing deep ignorance, blasphemy, or just looking very silly. In Indian tradition, those who imitate others are without true understanding of what they are doing. They have no real identity and are considered "fools". All the individuals we will review later, quoted by Sedonia Cahill and Bird Brother as teachers, are considered by real Indians as such fools and clowns. I have personally worked with hundreds of dreams of Indian men and women, and the images of "clowns" ("Heyokas" and "Mudheads") often occur in Indian dreams in relationship to white "wannabe" people. These dreams frequently depict those people as being very immature, unruly children and associated with clown figures and acts. They also appear as being dangerous, causing distress and wreaking havoc. In addition, the dreams emphasize the grief of Indian people and the necessity for women to protect the Pipe from such white children.

Indian people recognize that these individuals do not know who they are, have little sense of true identity, and need to borrow false names and false origins in order to impress others and obtain a following. Sedonia Cahill invokes the story of the Buffalo Calf Woman before her Pipe ceremonies on the vision quests, linking what she does to the tradition of the Sacred Pipe, which is specifically Lakota Sioux. The Buffalo Calf Woman brought a specific message to the Lakota people alone. Only part of the message is known to the general public. The ceremonies built around The Sacred Pipe have a context and a meaning for the Lakota people.

When she appeared upon the Plains, the Sioux were a Warrior Society with ancient war rituals. The Buffalo Calf Woman emerged from the collective psyche of the Plains Warrior Society, and is meaningful in that context. To take this event out of context, and to assign arbitrary meanings to it today is improper. If these people advanced that Moses brought corn to his people in the desert, or Jesus taught his disciples how to build an igloo, it would be just as ludicrous as to pretend that The Buffalo Calf Woman is watching over Sedonia Cahill's vision quests.

"Medicine" names, and the granting of honor feathers

At the conclusion of some of her ceremonies, Sedonia Cahill, like Harley Swift Deer at the end of his "Hoksida Rituals" or so-called "Sun Dances," often gives her customers an Indian name and a feather like a "prize." However, many of the questing clients take a name on their own. In Native American traditions, a name is bestowed, not self-given.

In real circumstances, Indian names are only bestowed upon non-Indians by Indians for specific, sustained and efficient work or contribution to an Indian community. An Indian name is an honor when it is thus acquired, meaningless if it is bestowed by a non-Indian such as Sedonia Cahill or Mr. Reagan. A feather is an honor which is rarely bestowed outside Indian circles. It acknowledges a specific contribution to the community, or a heroic deed for the protection of an Indian community. A feather and an Indian name given by a white woman to another white person carry no deep meaning. It is simply an imitative act without context or public communal significance. In Indian societies, the honor is a public honor, like a congressional medal. Socially, Sedonia Cahill's act has no such value. She, and many like her, imagines that this is a great spiritual gesture, not knowing that the real meaning of feather and name giving is social recognition.

Medicine Wheels and teachings

The terminology of The Great Round teachings is identical to that of Harley Swift Deer Reagan as worded in his Apprentice Manual. "Tonal" and "Nagual" shields are terms borrowed by both Mr. Reagan and Sedonia Cahill from Carlos Castenada. Castenada's work is not validated by Yaqui spiritual leaders (personal conversation between Helene Hagan and Alfonso Valencia, Spiritual Head, Pasquale Yaqui Reservation, Arizona), or in anthropological circles. Yet, Sedonia's reading list for vision quests includes his work, with the books of Lynn Andrews and others. Lynn Andrews has been instrumental in propagating the non-existent "Sisterhood of the Shields". She has been shown to peddle fantasy, and heads the list of "fake medicine people." The vision quest reading list also includes the writings of Jamake Highwater, a well-known Indian impersonator who actually was an Armenian ballet dancer in San Francisco.

Shields are associated with warrior paraphernalia and carry such a meaning in warrior societies of several nations of North America. They displayed honors obtained on the battlefield and were exhibited by the entrance of a tipi, as a coat of arms, so to speak. They carried no spiritual significance, but were held in great respect, for they depicted the high deeds of many valorous warriors. The making and use of shields by Sedonia Cahill and others is another misappropriation, distortion and abuse of meaningful Indian ways torn out of their contexts. The making of shields is part of Sedonia Cahill's and Bird Brother's teachings. There are many individuals in Northern California teaching the making of shields, as if it were an Indian ritual or ceremonial act of great spiritual significance.

The Sun Dance Ritual, the "Prune Dance," the "Flowering Tree Ceremony" and other such gatherings.

The specific indications that the teachings of the Great Round are connected to the practice of the Sun Dance which is strictly a Plains ceremony, is the statement on the part of one of the members of the group that some attend the Swift Deer Sun Dance, and a photograph from her recently published book. Such practice of the Sun Dance, without understanding the profound context of Lakota society and the place of this ritual in that context, is a travesty of a sacred ritual. The parody of a ritual, divested of its original intent within a given community where all ritual phases are interlinked in a specific way, is quite evident in the spurious sun dances held outside Indian communities.

The Medicine Wheel, which is used for ceremonies and the structure of the Vision Quest, is borrowed straight out of General Storm's book Seven Arrows, and is also at the core of all Deer Tribe teachings. Thus, Sedonia duly acknowledges Harley Swift Deer on page 15 of her book: "I give special thanks...to Harley Swift Deer for his beautiful and inspiring Medicine Wheel Teachings".

Other acts of desecration include the Vision Quest paraphernalia such as making tobacco ties, making prayer arrows, cornmeal offerings, imitations and borrowings from Indians in "playing Indian", buzzwords and symbols which grant an aura of "Indianness" to language and activities, for an appearance of authenticity.

Symbols

The Coyote Figure is displayed consistently in The Great Round Newsletter. The Coyote is a Native American trickster figure. It often is the first teacher, an intermediary between the higher spirit and mortals, particularly prominent in teachings for children. Coyote stories are morality tales like Aesop's Fables and constitute a Native American literary genre. This figure is demeaned by Sedonia, Bird Brother and The Great Round, and used as a cartoon prop speaking slang or poor English. For instance, A Spring 1989 newsletter includes the following poem:

ONE LAST COYOTE POEM-you like this newsletter? You wanna keep getting copies? You think this doesn't cost us anything? Hey, Sedonia needs your help...Please send some bucks if you haven't recently, to help pay for newsletter repro and mailing.

Activities

1. All ceremonies (pipe ceremonies, sweat lodges, vision quests, Indian chanting, and medicine circles).
2. Various instructions on "how to" : feather tying, making tobacco ties, making prayer arrows, making shields, making medicine bundles (including eagle feathers which are federally protected for use only by Native Americans), making amulets which include menstrual blood, pubic hair and fluids from genitalia.
3. Ancient gambling games like bone games.
4. Indian name giving, medicine name giving, honoring with feathers and using pipes. The use of the Pipe in a ceremonial way and the carrying of a pipe is by itself, without any other imitation or borrowing, a desecration of a ritual object sacred to the Plains people.

Based on the above list of linguistic habits, activities, symbols and publications, there is no doubt that Sedonia Cahill, Bird Brother and the organization of The Great Round, as do similar groups, present themselves to the public as teachers of Native American ways. They are indeed imitators, despite their claim to the contrary, to being "innovators and creators" of ritual, as put forward by Sedonia in her last publication (Summer 1992 Earth Circle News). "I have not known anyone in this community to copy ceremonies from any other people. We are innovators and creators." Such a statement does not need any further elaboration, in the light of the review of the activities just described. The pretense to innovation and the denial of imitation ring false. These phrases, activities, and ritual behavior have been learned from "teachers" whom they name in their publications. Almost all of these "teachers" are themselves non-Indian, often considered impersonators of Indians, and not trained in Native American traditional ways.

Expert and false teachers

'Teachers from these various traditions, including Native American teachers, have specifically shared rituals with the intent that they continue to be shared and taught". (Earth Circle News, Summer 1992 pg.3)

This statement is a double misrepresentation. Firstly, it refers to the "intent" of unnamed Native American teachers. There are no known real Native American Medicine Men and Women who have come forth in the non-Indian world to ask others to conduct and perpetuate Indian rituals and ceremonies. These ceremonies are performed by legitimate ritualists within their own communities for their own people. As noted elsewhere, some people have been invited to share these ceremonies, on and outside reservations, as participants and friends: they have always been specifically requested to respect their contents by not writing or talking about them publicly. This very matter is of crucial importance, and renders this statement by Alexandra Hart a falsification and distortion of reality. Secondly, in Native American circles, it is known that any Indian who has offered his teachings to outsiders was not a recognized spiritual leader of any nation, but had scant knowledge of the traditions. Such statements as put forth in the publications of The Great Round can only emanate from individuals who are not in communication with real American Indians.

Though it may seem that Sedonia Cahill, Bird Brother and the Great Round come recommended by a number of people, it is necessary to examine from whom the recommendations emanate. It is not unusual in those particular circles to find people who will praise such "plastic medicine people". Similarly, when Wilma Mankiller, Tribal President of the Cherokee Nation of Oklahoma, questioned the HBO producers of the Cherokee Sex Workshop featuring the work of Mr. Harley Swift Deer Reagan, their response was that Mr. Reagan had come highly recommended: "...staff checked with Mr. Reagan and accepted a lot of reference material he provided, but did not check with the Cherokee Nation to find out if he was a legitimate medicine man or if the workshops he conducts are Cherokee sexual spiritual ceremonies as he claims....He has been doing these teachings for years. He has a very huge following." (Lakota Times, Article on Cherokee Workshop, Jan. 21, 1992).

Harley Reagan is only one of the several teachers Sedonia acknowledges in her writings and in her reading list for the preparation of her clients to the vision quest. There are also other comments by people who attend her circles, such as made by Harri Meyers in the above Lakota Times report of Jan 21, 1992. "Those who have studied Native American religions have studied with Harley Swift Deer. Several circle members studied with Mr. Reagan and go to Sun Dance with them, Mr. Meyers said." Also available is an Uvideo of the Cherokee Sex Workshop conducted by Mr. Reagan and shown by HBO for which the Cherokee Nation is demanding an apology on the part of its producers, and equal air time to offset the false impression on Indian authenticity.

Since information has recently come out publicly discrediting Mr. Reagan, Bird Brother has stated that he and Sedonia hardly know Harley Swift Deer have had little to do with his teachings, and did one weekend workshop ten years ago. This statement and the bulk of information available on the link between The Great Round teachings and the Deer Tribe do not coincide.

I have already commented on Sun Bear, Carlos Castaneda, Lynn Andrews and Harley Swift Deer. I have also mentioned the background role of Hyemeyohsts "General Storm" who is denied authenticity by Indians, and Jamake Highwater, the Armenian ballet dancer impersonating a Blackfoot/Crow Indian. Other false teachers mentioned by Sedonia Cahill are: Evelyn Eaton, O'Shinna "Fast Wolf" and Shequish Ohoho.

a. **Evelyn Eaton** was a "medicine woman" of the Bear Tribe and of the Harley Swift Deer Tribe (both non-Indian groups). She also spoke admiringly of General Storm in her book, *The Shaman & The Medicine Wheel*. Evelyn Eaton was a fiction writer with some twenty-three published *novels*.

b. **O'Shinna "Fast Wolf"** is of Irish and Scottish ancestry, and is currently impersonating an Indian woman of Native American ancestry which switches from Mohawk to Sioux to Apache according to the occasion. Her name was taken without permission from Calvin Fast Wolf, a Lakota man she encountered in Chicago. Furthermore she has been thoroughly investigated by Avis Little Eagle of the Lakota Times, who could not find any Indian lineage or tribal affiliation.

c. **Shequish Ohoho** is interviewed by Sedonia Cahill as part of her recent book, on pages 107-113: "She is a warrior woman of Shumash Indian ancestry. She is a very articulate teacher drawing on her own roots, Hopi and Apache training." I personally know

Shequish. I also know that she came to the attention of Native American people two years ago as an impostor who pretended to have Shumash ancestry. I received a personal telephone call and a letter from the Chairman of a Shumash group south of Monterey. This phone call and a letter followed a Council meeting in which Shumash people took the decision to put a stop to Shequish Ohoho's activities in the Bay area as an "Indian woman."

A group of real Indian women of San Francisco led a protest against Shequish and effectively terminated her money making seminars and ceremonies in this area. Her real name and background are known to California Indians who have denied her any tribal affiliation.

Most of the teachers mentioned by Sedonia Cahill and Bird Brother are non-Indians, without tribal affiliation, and some are simply impersonating Indians with fake identities. At one point all have had some involvement with Sun Bear, a discredited Indian, or with Harley Swift Deer, a known "plastic medicine man" under coast-to-coast scrutiny. If these are the teachers Sedonia Cahill and Bird Brother hold in reverence, it is easy to establish that they are self-appointed teachers of no known Indian roots. Moreover, the majority of these people are known to Indians for having assumed false identities or promulgating improper teachings.

Whatever is based on false identity cannot pretend to truth. The source of Native American spirituality is strong identity, knowing who you are and acting straight from the core of your individuality. Mental health is linked to truth and identity, and the very problems emerging from western societies in the form of mental breakdown, neuroses and psychoses, are caused by some form of lie at family or social levels. Whatever starts with an untruth cannot heal. Mental illness or health, truth and identity are fundamentally linked. A false identity cannot lead to mental health.

Issues/Points of difference

"Certainly the Earth-centered movement is growing into its own use of ritual and healing techniques which have all the eclectic roots of our own melting-pot heritage, and have at their center perhaps more to do with current psychological knowledge than any other tradition." (Alexandra Hart, pg 3, Summer 1992 of Earth Circle News.)

Like Bird Brother and Sedonia Cahill, the people in such networks all purport to have a spiritual calling and to be legitimately trained in one or more Native American traditions. The fact of the matter is that they are not legitimate in the eyes of any Native American community, nor do they hold any seminar, conference or ceremonies among Native Americans. What they have in common is that they steer away from real Indians, do not interact with them and absolve themselves of any responsibility toward the Native American community, locally or nationally.

Furthermore, some have the audacity to claim that the Native American medicine people and elders are "jealous" of their "powers" (comment by O'Shinna Fast Wolf in the same issue), a ridiculous notion which only reflects the low level of esteem such commentators hold for Native American spiritual leaders and elders who are concerned about the proliferation of fake medicine people. Such statements deny Native American intelligence and wisdom, and ignore the very real possibility that legitimate traditionalists would know how dangerous the manipulation of partial ceremonial knowledge can be to the individual and collective psyches.

Traditionalists know how damaging someone who is not trained properly can be when manipulating psychic forces or invoking spirits of the depths without adequate preparation. It is this knowledge which impels the real spiritual Indian leaders to warn against these "plastic medicine people", whether they call themselves "medicine" men and women, "shamans" or any other name. No Indian spiritual leader speaks of ownership of spirit, as they have been accused of recently in publications of The Great Round, as such notion is idiotic. To even advance such a notion can only stem from very ignorant people in matters of Native American spirituality. It also reeks of racism, for it belittles the intelligence of a group of people in such a way that can only be called racist.

When Sedonia and Bird Brother write or speak about ownership of spirit, they are showing childish ignorance of spiritual matters. Indians are not seeking to protect their ceremonies from being practiced by others who hold more "power". The issue of power is a very misunderstood one, indeed. It is one that involves the shadow of all individuals engaged in the healing professions in the western world. To know how to relinquish power is the first step to spiritual understanding and the step missing from all New Age Indian teachings. People are getting very rich indeed in misleading others into quests for "powers" toward false values.

Rather, Indians are concerned that bits and pieces of their ceremonies are used and manipulated without discretion, in an ignorant manner as to their consequences. They are concerned that such actions, based on slavish imitation and improprieties, can cause damage to others, and that the very people who speak so loudly of their concern for mental health are engaging in unauthentic spiritual practices. Psychic damage has been known to result from such experiences. The individual may not be able to link it directly and it may show up in unpredictable ways months and years later. Native American spiritual leaders are fully aware of these dangers.

To belittle the knowledge of Indians, and to pretend that their practices can be taken over by non-Indians harmlessly are indications of non understanding and arrogance. To fabricate new ceremonies out of bits and pieces of various Indian rituals, out of the full ritual context in which they are embedded, is to create psychic monstrosities. This, the fake medicine people are unaware of. Rituals have a context. They are a part of an entire fabric of a given society, and one ritual is only a part of a whole. The balance is in the whole, not in the parts. And the whole is still the full practice within Indian circles, founded on ancient Indian traditions, for Indian people. Others can pretend to achieve identical results with only outward paraphernalia and a patchwork of gleaned information as to the steps of certain rites, but they do not have the key to the whole meaning, the whole context, and how the parts complement and fit each other. They are crippling other human beings by subjecting them to only bits or parts of a whole system, without having the keys to the entire mental system.

This is truly what is at stake and why Indians are concerned. They know these people do not have a clue and through arrogance, greed for money, for results, for power, for prestige, for followers, for validation of their fantasy trips, or from simple ignorance engage in improper behavior. As to the claim that rituals are "generic" and not specific to any group of people, one must indeed be a trained anthropologist to speak to that issue. Sedonia and Bird Brother are not. Rituals have contexts, are context specific and emerge from the collective unconscious of a particular group.

There are patterns which are embedded in an ecosystem, particular to a given culture and which function precisely and effectively for a particular group. It is Theodore Rosack who emphasizes that we are on the verge of discovering that the deep unconscious is not just sexual (Freud), or spiritual (Jung), but related to the ecosystem in which we live. And in that regard we must understand how Western people have diverged very far indeed from their unconscious in a destructive way. The destruction of the environment goes hand in hand with the destruction of our relationship to the unconscious, which is at its very depth our natural habitat and its indigenous populations. The recovery of this relatedness of all things can be accomplished as individuals, simply, genuinely and honestly without external trappings or borrowed traditions.

Rituals have to do with the careful relationship to these depths and ways have developed among certain people to balance these forces which can affect the individual and collective mental health of a given group. Playing with rituals is a dangerous game and in this regard Westerners who play at being Indians are unaware and unconscious. That is why Indians are concerned. Such "plastic medicine people" are fooling around with mental health and in ways for which they are not properly trained by experts. It is not a question of dispute over who is right and who is wrong and who owns spirituality.

Furthermore, the views set forth by The Great Round publications that "rituals are generic" and can be borrowed from one group or another and passed around reflects abysmal ignorance as to the very specific qualities of ritual as it is elaborated by the collective psyche of a given group of people, and it is valid for them alone. No ritual can be borrowed. No ritual can be created as an innovation by one individual. In indigenous groups, innovation occurs only as it emerges from a vision or a dream of a member of that community and bears all the marks of having a collective meaning, and must pass the scrutiny of experts in that community. The contention, for instance, that the "Prune Dance" began to be practiced by these New Age people because some white man dreamt of the world as if it were dried up like a prune and therefore needed a new ceremony to juice it up, is a severe misunderstanding of the true nature of dream. That white man's dream referred to his white world and not to any Sun Dance, which is an Indian ceremony. It might have meant that this particular man's environment was like a dried prune. The white man's arrogance is boundless.

And while indeed the Spirit exists for each and all, and manifests in many ways, the way a human group relates to the earth is very specific. Each ritual, item, song or action exists in a very real context of family and social life in a group, and carries meaning within this very group, and not for other people. To borrow bits and pieces and create some hodgepodge for one's own benefit, financial or emotional, and as one wishes, is indeed the American way, but it is also very sad. It is as if Americans were so spiritually bankrupt that they did not have any inner resources to draw from and had to borrow from others the source of any inspiration. To peddle such hodgepodge to others for a fee, be it vision quest, sweat lodge or other ceremony, is taking advantage of the gullible and disoriented and to profit by it. This is the true essence of charlatanism.

In Native American traditions, the holy men and women, the spiritual advisors and medicine people hold different functions in society and have very different training. But all are sustained by their community without benefit to themselves. In return, they know that their primary responsibility is to their community, and should they depart from that path, seeking fame or glory or financial gain, they are leaving their true vocation and will be shunned. True humility and service to others are indeed their remarkable qualities. They do not market themselves, do not publicize their skills and do not issue flyers. They work hard in silence and in true dedication to the welfare of others and they know well the dark forces which can overcome them should they depart from their obligations.

Indian medicine men and women train from childhood. They are not allowed to practice until they have undergone a long experience of the powerful spirits or psychic forces they will encounter first in themselves, long before they are singled out for specific healing tasks by others. They do not appoint themselves. Rarely does a medicine man or woman come to practice before maturity, for these very reasons. There is not a hint of this wisdom in any of the so-called teachings passed around in the "circles" forming around plastic medicine people.

Conclusion

My contention has been that these individuals and the organizations they head at times represent themselves as purveyors of authentic Native American teachings-which they definitely are not-and sometimes as creators and innovators of important rituals gathered from various traditions (not uniquely Native American). Sedonia and Bird Brother have also advanced at times that in ancient European traditions there were sweat lodges and medicine circles, and that they are therefore only reviving old traditions from their own Caucasian origins. If so, then, why do they use American Indian language and paraphernalia at all? The contention that sweat lodges and vision quests existed long ago among Celtic or Nordic people is not verifiable. There is no continuity of tradition in this regard in Europe. And if there is in their mind, they must adhere to the European mode of conducting these ceremonies and follow these Caucasian ways. Spirituality is embedded in language and collective memory. The fact is that no Westerner, European or Caucasian carries in his or her psyche the collective memory of American Indians of this continent. To pretend to that memory is a blatant falsehood which cannot be maintained. Both common sense and scholarly expertise recognize such falsehood.

Helene E. Hagan is a psychological anthropologist who has worked with Native American issues for over a decade. She lived for four years on the Pine Ridge Reservation in South Dakota while working on an elder oral history project. This article is reprinted with permission from the INSTITUTE OF ARCHETYPAL ETHNOLOGY newsletter September 1990.

ST. VINCENT AND SILVEIRA RANCH ETHNOGRAPHIC REPORT

Marin County, November 22, 1994

The Saint Vincent and the Silveira Ranch properties are located in Marin County, north of the City of San Rafael. They are considered together for the purpose of this report. They consist of two adjacent pieces of land which were originally part of the Mexican Rancho Grant of San Pedro, Santa Margarita y Las Gallinas given to Timothy Murphy (1834 Map of lands belonging to Mission San Rafael Archangel, Bancroft, History of California.)

As other mission lands, these properties were first used by the Spanish missionaries to raise crops and cattle to support the mission. According to a description of Mission San Rafael, cattle grazed in "the canadas of Las Gallinas." Another range under the supervision of the priests was named Santa Margarita.

While the site of the mission itself was the Indian village of Nana Guanui, the site under consideration in this report was the village of Chotomkot'cha.

GENERAL ARCHAEOLOGICAL FEATURES IN MARIN COUNTY *from Nelson (Heizer, 1-14:157)*

"From San Rafael northward nearly every ravine and every gully appears to have offered attractions. But the great majority of the mounds are situated on or near the small streams, though with considerable indifference, it seems, as to whether the surrounding country is barren plain or timbered hills. Wherever a group of separate deposits line a stream, it is not unusual to find the largest accumulations at the lower end of the series, and some mounds are found out in the salt marsh."

"...The shell mounds are confined in a narrow belt around the open waters of the bay and grade off landward into earth mounds."

"Another fact which drew attention to the deposits was a frequently accompanying growth of buckeyes (Aesculus Californicus)... It is well known that the Indians of recent times prepared the large bitter nuts of this tree for food. They are said, moreover, to have used its soft wood for making fires and to have believed in the medicinal virtues of its bark."

EARLY MIWOK - ARCHAEOLOGICAL FINDINGS

Draft of City of San Rafael Plan:

"Miller Creek meanders through the northern section of the Silveira Ranch property and the southern portion of St. Vincent's. Dense clumps of willow (Salix) and Himalaya blackberry line some sections of the creek, while other sections are characterized by low benches covered with herbs, grasses and rushes. Along the western section of the Miller Creek, near its junction with Highway 101, the creek banks support valley and coast live oaks, California bay laurel, white alder and California buckeye. Livestock use has denuded several areas of both sides of the creek.

S-11546 - Sonoma County Archaeological Center:

"More than ten shell midden sites were recorded by Nelson during his examination of Miller Creek."

S-12801 - Sonoma County Archaeological Center - Michael J. Moratto:

"There is evidence of occupation in the region for at least 10,000 years."

Charles Slaymaker (1974 - SF State)

"The ethnographic Historical Village of Chotomko'tca located within Las Gallinas Valley coincides with large site clusters noted by Nelson and others along Miller Creek and Las Gallinas Creek. Since the greatest population density occurs along Miller Creek which enters the bay at a point four and a half miles north of San Rafael, it is assumed that the site cluster recorded along Miller Creek represents the settlement of Chotomko'tca." (Page 125)

"The location of the village of Ewu, one and a half miles south of Miller Creek... (was) a subsidiary settlement within the tribelet of Chotomko'tca."

The Slaymaker Study illustrates the continuity of Coast Miwok culture from archaeological to historical and ethnographic periods as the tribe of Chotomko'tca which controlled all lands within the Gallinas Valley drainage system.

A number of Coast Miwok tribelets lived north of the Golden Gate Bridge to the Bay Shore, where food was abundant and diversified. The Coast Miwok fished, hunted and gardened alongside the Miller Creek and the natural boundary of the Petaluma river, seeking subsistence alongside the San Francisco Bay, in the inland valleys, and the Pacific coastline, occupying all of the region now designated on maps as Marin County and Southern Sonoma County. These tribes shared a cultural complex known to historians as Coast Miwok. The Coast Miwok were distributed throughout the area, and large seasonal camps and villages were formed from Sausalito to Hamilton Air Force Base alongside The Miller Creek drainage system which was the site of an important settlement of Coast Miwok people of the Chotomkotcha tribe (Ethnographic Field Notes on the Coast Miwok Indians, Kelly, 1932, Manuscript on file at Bancroft Library, University of California, Berkeley.)

Early maps record the presence of the village. The earliest archaeological survey of the area (Nelson, 1906) identifies a number of sites along the Miller Creek to the Bay Shore. N. C. Nelson made the following observations in his 1906 survey of the area, one that he indicates as incomplete and preliminary (Helier 144, 1957):

"The great majority of the mounds are situated on or near the small streams... Wherever a group of separate deposits line a stream it is usual to find the largest accumulations at the lower end of the series ... some mounds are found out in the salt marshes." Nelson identified several sites along the Miller Creek lower end as it reaches the Bay Shore, on the present locations of the St. Vincent and Silveira properties.

In 1977, Charles Slaymaker prepared an extensive archaeological document on the area and wrote:

"The ethnographic/historical village of Chotomkot'cha, located within the Gallinas Valley coincides with large site clusters positioned by Nelson and others along Miller Creek and Gallinas Creek. Since the greatest population density occurs along Miller Creek which enters the bay at a point four and a half miles north of San Rafael, it is assumed that the site cluster recorded along Miller Creek represents the settlement of Chotomkot'cha." (Page 125, Slaymaker, 1977) See also M. A. P. 0. M. Paper No. 3 entitled "The Material Culture of Chotornicoecha" - Moratto (1984). which cites evidence of the Coast Miwok occupation in the region for at least 10,000 years.

Slaymaker also explored the potential of bay marshes for Coast Miwok subsistence. He stated that the salt marsh association links the eastern margin of the Gallinas Valley to the waters of the San Pablo Bay (page 136, 1977): "Although extensively drained and filled for reclamation purposes, remnants of this association exist where Miller Creek flows into the Bay. Coast Miwok used mussels and oysters found in the salt marsh to craft shell beads which have an enormous importance in the understanding of California Indian life styles. Artifacts accompanying some of the clam disc beads suggest the survival of a distinct Coast Miwok style into the nineteenth century in Marin County. The Bead Complex of Central California is defined by the Coast Miwok specimens. These people were probably the inventors and initial developers of this craft type. Everywhere in Marin County, clam disc beads are temporal indicators of the Late Horizon Phase, dating Coast Miwok cultural continuity from the thirteenth century to the nineteenth century."

Slaymaker indicated that "primary or subsidiary settlements may have their residential structures spread along a creek or a river, on both sides, for over a mile and still be considered one settlement or village." This view is sustained by other archaeologists. The definition of village (Kroeber, 1925) refers to a tract of land rather than a settlement as such. In most cases, the population scattered throughout this tract in several settlements, with one central site considered as "principal." All studies show that a group of settlements located within a natural drainage system constituted such a village. Tribelets were in control of small territories located on the valley floors along suitable streams or creeks.

Archaeologists were prevented from entering the Silveira Ranch property in more recent decades. However, a number of documents reflect the concern of some archaeologists. In 1982, David Chavez examined the area (Las Gallinas Sanitary District), and paid special attention to the Nelson sites. "A review of archaeological site maps shows a major concentration of prehistoric sites is recorded in Las Gallinas Valley, along the banks of the Miller Creek. More than ten midden sites were recorded by Nelson during his examination of Miller Creek... The closest sites are MEN 132, 133 and 134 on the south sides of the creek. These sites are located downstream of where Miller Creek is crossed by the State Highway and the railroad crossing on the east. All these sites are located on the Silveira property. This parcel has never been systematically examined since Nelson's visit in 1907, principally because the land has not been developed and remains in agricultural use."

Flyn and Roop (1984) also indicated the presence of small vernal pool areas on the Silveira ranch, stating that grinding implements, mortars and charm stones might be found in that area, as aboriginal settlements often were established near marshes or grasslands. They consider that the presence of an isolated charm stone in the uppermost part of the Smith Ranch Hills parcel may be related to possible prehistoric use of the vernal pool depressions of the larger village site on that section of Miller Creek running through the Silveira property. They remark that "characteristic topography of vernal pools has revealed in similar physiological settings of the Sacramento and San Joaquim valleys prehistoric activity linked to vernal pools."

Koch and Potter (1987) found a Franciscan chart drill point on the Smith Ranch Hill parcel. They indicate that the discovery of the drill near the location of an isolated charm stone found in 1979 strongly suggests that other tools may be present.

"Since this tool is located in the same general area as the sandstone charm stone found in 1979, its discovery confers a greater significance to the area than unusual. What may be represented by the charm stone and the chert drill is a trail alignment cresting the hill separating the Las Gallinas on the north from the Santa Margarita Valley on the south."

Principal Documents:

Slaymaker (1974): San Francisco State M. A. Thesis "Miller Creek Site."

S. Van Dyke (1972): San Francisco M. A. Thesis "Settlement Patterning in Prehistoric Marin County" - 1956 Main Report on the ownership, occupation and use of the land surface and shores of California by the Indians, Manuscript prepared for U. S. Indian Land Claim Commission.

Dietz and Jackson (1973a): "An Archaeological Impact Survey of the Proposed Smith Ranch Development in the vicinity of Las Gallinas, Marin County" - San Francisco State.

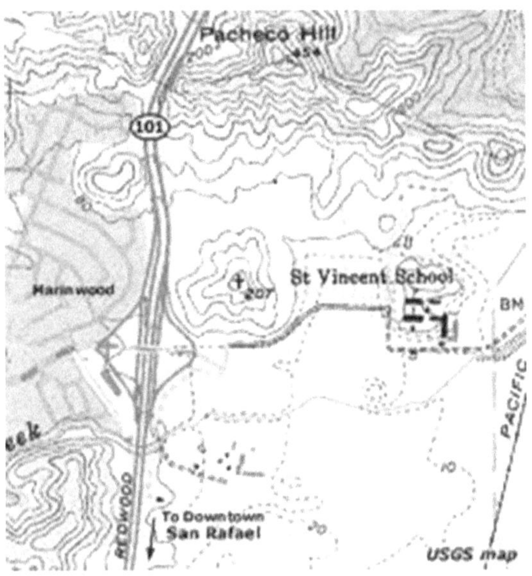

EARLY HISTORY

The Oral History of the living descendants of the inhabitants of this ancient village reflects knowledge of stories attached to this particular site, half a century after the arrival of the Spanish missionaries. Greg Sarris, the Elected Chair of the Federated Coast Miwok people, descends from the group which occupied the land in question and is a well-known writer and story teller. He has personal knowledge of stories related to the area of the Miller Creek and his ancestral village.

In addition, we have nineteenth century written documents referring to the presence of Miwok groups living on that property up until 1848, time at which an epidemic of small-pox decimated the group and what was left of it took refuge in the hills of what is now mapped as Southern Sonoma County.

The attached Historical Bibliography from the Mission era and the Days of the Mexican Dons is too ample to review. A few excerpts are offered. The only independent account of the life of the San Rafael Mission was given by a Russian, Otto Von Kotzeben, who visited the mission in the 1820's, accompanied by a Spanish settler, Don Estudillo. His report, unlike church reports, is untainted by religious fervor or bias: "No native ever presented himself freely to the missionaries. The friars sent out dragoons who lassoed the gentiles and drag them back to the missions half dead. The friars were solely intent on their private gain. They enriched themselves here by the mere labor imposed upon their converts and they return to Spain with their treasures." The Russian further indicates that the Marin Mission had "much more the appearance of a defensive outpost than the other missions."

General Mariano Vallejo's extensive amount of documents is preserved in the Bancroft Library at U.C. Berkeley, for the most part in microfilm. Vallejo documented the conquest of northern California and the military era which succeeded the missionary era. He wrote: 'The Indians practiced the arts taught them by friars. They were the ones who tended the vegetables and tended the orchards. They made the adobe and kept it in repair. It was they who skinned the carcass and butchered it and melted the fat and dried the meat and worked the rawhides. The Indians would do the labor."

Some of the accounts concerning the friars are less than edifying. Father Quijas (1834-1839), in particular, was a disgrace to his church. There is the 19th century anecdote (Hansen and Miller, 1962) relating how Father Quijas and his Irish friend, Timothy Murphy, visited Fort Ross to get brandy and got arrested and jailed in Sonoma. Quijas is reported in many accounts as having taken to drink "and no longer kept his vows." Another story (Vallejo) describes him as having such a conduct toward Reed's wife that "she fled into the woods rather than stay with him. On his return, Reed found the priest drunk. The friar tried to stab Reed with a knife and crumbled down crying."

Charles Lauff describes Timothy Murphy as typical of an era of dons living in luxury. When the missions were secularized, Timothy Murphy who by then called himself Don Timoteo Murphy, took over the mission lands and the care of the Indian servants and cattlemen. Timothy Murphy had aspired to the hand of Vallejo's sister and was turned down. He remained a bachelor. Charles Lauff writes: "Murphy had several nice looking Indian women around the house and numerous servants." The Rancho economy was based on a peonage of Indians. Domesticated Indians continued to be a cheap source of labor. The entire work force consisted of Indians who were no better than slaves. James Karats (Indians of California, page 21) wrote: "The rancheros ruled as lords on their great landed estates and the Indian worker who tended the fields and lands were their serfs." John Marsh (1836, page 77) stated: "throughout all California, the Indians are the principal laborers; without them the business of the country could hardly be carried on."

Charles Lauff documents the epidemics which devastated the Miwok Indian population around San Rafael. I will quote his remarks extensively as they give an account of what happened to the Coast Miwok of Marin County in mid-century. On pages 16 and 17, Charles Lauff records:

"In the early part of 1837, a party of Russian soldiers who were located at Fort Ross became ill with smallpox. The disease broke among the Indians, and before the end of the year, over 300 Indians were buried in the rancheros of Marin and Sonoma counties... The Indians died so fast that they covered the ground for miles around, and the Mexican officers were compelled to have the bodies buried in deep holes and covered over. Many of the tribes deserted San Rafael, going into Sonoma and Napa counties."

"Another small tribe of Indians who wintered near Olompali or Burden's would spend the Indian summer where McNear had his home near McNear's Point. In 1848 and 1849, there was a fine clam bed where the Municipal Baths now stand. In fact, you could dig clams in any portion of the lowlands in East San Rafael, as the tides covered all of the lowlands at that time... This tribe of Indians was the same that attacked Mission San Rafael years before. Their principal ranchero was at Burdell's Station. There were several hundred Indians in the tribe."

In 1836, a few hundred were located at San Quentin Point and McNear's Point. "The remainder settled in Miller Valley and Nicasio Valley." On page 70, Lauff indicates that "In the camp at the foot of B Street over 500 Indians died from the smallpox and were buried in the block surrounded by Taylor, South C and Bayview Streets. Over 1,200 Indians died in San Rafael alone. I was told by the fathers that they sent Indians to Nicasio where 300 were buried in the ranchero. In Miller Valley over 200 Indians died."

The 1918 narrative of Steve Richardson entitled 'The Days of the Don" contains good documentation regarding the presence and life styles of the Miwok Indians during his childhood and adolescent days. His evaluation of historical facts is often sharp. Regarding the fall of Mission

San Rafael, he writes: "Other versions have been given of the downfall of the missions. This is the story in compact form: it was *a gigantic land deal,* nothing more." Richardson notes that the building and maintenance of the mission grounds was the hard work of Miwok people, and that the "Well-trained domestic staff was nearly all Indians."

Steve Richardson writes (pages 29-30): "We talk about those stately buildings mostly ruins now that dot the coastline from San Diego to old Sonoma as the work of the Spaniards. Rubbish! They were the work of the Indians inside and out, from start to finish. Among these Indians I have known in person were skillful carpenters, masons, blacksmiths, cabinet makers, metal workers, experts with many kinds of tolls... Believe me, if it had been left to the Spaniards, they would have been no Missions... Outside of mechanical and structural pursuits, the Indians raised wheat corn, and other grains, tended sheep, kept a lookout on the cattle, cultivated the soil for small fruits and vegetables, and caught an abundance of fish."

It is also important to document that the earliest use of water in Marin County, before and after the arrival of a white population, was made by Coast Miwok Indians. The Jones Memorandum (1851), a Report to the Secretary of the Interior, states on page 115 that 'The woods of this mission are composed of oaks, live oaks, and other productive trees raised from seeds planted by the Indians." Water rights, according to western water laws, belong to the ones who first made productive use of those waters. All accounts record that the Coast Miwok were the first to do so in Marin County and therefore technically hold all water rights in and around San Rafael mission lands and cattle ranch, which include the St. Vincent property and the Silveira ranch property.

The short vignettes related here are by no means an extensive account of the era of the mission and the era of Mexican rule. Interested readers can consult the attached bibliography for further readings.

The Mexican land Grants

The most exhaustive document on the little understood subject of the tenure of land in California is a report on land titles in California by William Carey Jones published in Washington in 1850 on instructions from the Secretary of State and the Secretary of the Interior. Mr. Jones was a government appointed investigator on the condition of land titles in

California at that time. From this report, examining the different types of Mexican land grants, there is a careful review of the special case of large land grants of the Missions; the report emphasizes that the missionaries never had any other rights than those of occupation and use of the lands for the purposes of the missions, and at the pleasure of the government. "This is shown by the history of the Government toward them, and, in fact, by the rules of the Franciscan order, which forbids its members to possess property."

The Dominican friars obtained leave from the King to take charge of a part of the missions in California, which led to an arrangement between the two societies, whereby the missions of lower California were committed to the Dominicans, and the entire field of the upper provinces remained to the Franciscans.'

Indian rights and The Treaty of Guadelupe Hidalgo (1848)

The memorandum of W. C. Jones also states that "I am also instructed to make an enquiry into the nature of Indian Rights in the soil under the Spanish and Mexican governments."

"It is a principle constantly laid down in the Spanish colonial laws, that the Indians shall have a right to so much land as they need for their habitations, for tillage, and for pasturage."

"..Agreeably to the theory and spirit of these laws, the Indians in California were always supposed to have a certain property or interest in the missions... But apart from any direct grant, they have been always reckoned to have a right of settlement; and we shall find that all the plans that have been adopted for the secularization of the missions, have contemplated, recognized, and provided for this right." In the Treaty of Guadelupe Hidalgo, the Senate removed wholesale from Article DC all reference to religion, the Catholic Church or its property by a vote of 31 to 16 on March 7, 1848. The American government did not provide any special privilege or protection for the property rights of the Catholic Church in the new territories, and the Church found itself having to fight for her case before the American courts.

Jose de Jesus Gonzalez Rubio

He was the administrator of the diocese of Monterey upon the death in 1846 of the Mexican prelate, Bishop Garcia y Moreno. Gonzalez Rubio was "the living link between the Mexican and the American church in California, and universally considered the most respected Catholic churchman in California before the arrival of Bishop Alemany." (The Archbishop Claim, Harry B. Morrison)

The view of the Catholic Church regarding Indian rights is best spelled out in a letter from Rubio, as Vicar General, to Father John B. Brouillet, dated June 23, 1849. In that letter, Gonzalez Rubio stated emphatically that the mission lands never belonged to anyone except the Indians and that the Church could not and should not press a legal claim to property in her own name.

The Appointment of Joseph Sardoc Alemany to California.

Joseph Alemany was Spanish born and was in Naples when the American Catholic Church began to look for an English speaking bishop to take over the task of the claim of the missions in California. In December 1849, the Pope named Bishop Montgomery to the post of Monterey, a position which Montgomery refused. It was then that Joseph Alemany was considered, and in June 30 1850, he was consecrated at Rome Bishop of Monterey. The task of the Bishop was to secure the property rights of the Church in California.

Upon his arrival in Santa Barbara on December 30, 1850, Bishop Alemany officially took charge of the diocese record known as the *LIBRO BARRADOR*. This book, he judged, would be "devoted to the Records of my Official diocesan business as Bishop of Monterey." This official business, that of securing the mission lands, fills the great majorities of the entries of this book, particularly the legal process to obtain clear title to the mission lands. He officially recorded in the Libro Barrador the nature of this diocesan business:

"The Old Franciscan Missionaries explain to me that the tracts of the Mission lands were, as they believed, the real property of the Indians, who cultivated the same under their direction, and more especially under their alcaldes, or chief Indian Officers, elected by the Indians themselves, and acting under the direction of the Fathers. But that the Churches, Church edifices, stores, cemeteries, orchards, and vineyards with aqueducts should be considered the property of the Church." (Libro, page 144)

Alemany learned that no formal grant of title had ever been made to the Church itself for the lands and properties at the missions. He began to seek advice, and governmental allies. The California Land Act of 1851 set the judicial procedure which Bishop Alemany and all other Californians who claimed private land titles would have to follow. It put the burden of proof on the claimant, and the commissioners were "to be governed by the Treaty of Guadeloupe Hidalgo, the law of nations, the laws, usages, and customs of the government from which the claim is derived, the principles of equity, and the decisions of the supreme Court of the United States, so far as they are applicable." (U. S. Statutes at Large IX: 631) The Amended California Land Act of 1852 tightened the appeal process. Under this Amendment, the Federal Government was to appeal automatically all decisions made in favor of the claimants. In other words, the Federal Government which had agreed through the Treaty of Guadelupe Hidalgo that the property of the residents of the annexed territories would be inviolably respected, had, by 1852, reserved to itself the right to oppose any and every private land claim in the State of California. There were two California Court districts, a southern one, and a northern one. The United States District Court for the Northern District of California was established on September 28, 1850, only two years after California was ceded to the United States by Mexico in 1848 by the Treaty of Guadalupe Hidalgo and less than three weeks after California's statehood on September 9, 1850. California's first two federal courts (established simultaneously) divided the state into two districts, southern and northern.

In Section 16 of the Land Act of 1852, the Commissioners are specifically enjoined to ascertain and report to the Secretary of the Interior the tenure by which the mission lands are held as well as those of the missionized Indians. Such was the judicial procedure presented to Bishop Alemany. The process is all important in the unique case of the Alemany Land Claim which, as we shall see below, was not appealed by the federal government in the Northern Court District of California, as mandated by law, through political influence exercised by the Bishop of San Francisco over one Attorney General. The decision not to appeal was reversed by his successor, too late, however, to be effective in the

Northern District Court. It is important to emphasize the uniqueness of the situation in the Annals of the California Claims, and its departure from the Law of the Land as stipulated in the Land Act of 1852. One step was omitted in the judicial procedure. There was no U.S. Appeal in the case which was adjudicated in the northern district court of California, though such Appeal had been mandated by law. Therefore, the decision which ruled in favor of Bishop Alemany and the Catholic Church for mission lands north of Santa Barbara circumvented the procedure established by the Congress of the United States, was unconstitutional, and remains so in the record.

The Joseph Alemany Land Grant

The Bishop retained a "good conscientious Catholic lawyer" by the name of Eugene Casserly (a New Yorker), but it was the Bishop himself who steered the politics of the case, and made all decisions.

The Bishop was faced with several possibilities. Under Section 16 of the 1852 Act, he could rely upon a favorable decision to the commissioners' report mandated by law on mission lands and missionized Indians. Or he could make his own petition to the Board of Land Commissioners for confirmation of his claim to specific properties of each mission, subjecting oneself to the same process as all other claimants. Or, he could, citing the special character of the claim in question, circumvent the whole process by making an extraordinary petition to Congress.

Bishop Alemany convened a Synod of priests in March 1853 to adopt a resolution concerning the mission lands, which specifically referred to the churches, cemeteries, houses, and gardens of the missions as well as ecclesiastical property belonging to the church, and, in addition, one section of land at each mission for the Church and one square league at each mission for the Indians.

The Archbishop of San Francisco put forth his claim for the mission lands of California as an individual, incorporated solo. He carefully constructed his claim around the issue of the need for the Catholic Church to obtain some of the mission lands for the purpose of establishing "Seminaries", that is ecclesiastical institutions for young men to enter Holy Orders, and specifically - as recommended by the California Synod of Priests - included in the language of the claim the recognition that only land needed for seminaries were sought, the rest remaining in the title of local Indians, namely One Square league of each mission remaining in the title of Indians. Casserly and Doyle, the Attorneys for the Archbishop filed Alemany's claim to the lands of the Catholic Church on February 19, 1853 as claim number 609 before the board. On February 28 they filed Alemany's claim for one square league of each mission on behalf of the Indians of California, claim number 663. (Archbishop Alemany filed the claim of the Church with the Land Commission on February 19, 1853 (Case No. 609). Confirmation by the Commission took place December 18, 1855. It is registered as Case No. 425 in the Northern District Court records of California land claims. The appeal to the District Court was dismissed March 16, 1857, Northern District, and March 15, 1858, Southern District (Case Nos. 425, N.D. and 388, S.D.). Patents for each mission area were issued to Archbishop J. S. Alemany.)

The question of Section 16 of the Land Act of 1851 which required the board to submit to the Secretary of the Interior a report on the status of the mission lands was one which worried the Archbishop deeply. Archbishop Alemany communicated with the Secretary of the Interior, putting emphasis on the fact that the claim at issue was not one for the "large tracts" of a square league at each mission for the Indians, but rather the claim for "only some small parcels besides two moderate grants, all of which I consider to be church property distinct from the Mission lands of the Indians."

After reviewing the ecclesiastical character of the use to which the buildings and lands claimed were put, one of the three Commissioners, Alpheus Felch, stated the essence of the case and concluded:

"These concurrent proofs bring us irresistibly to the conclusion that before the treaty of Guadelupe Hidalgo, these possessions were solemnly dedicated to the use of the Church, and the property withdrawn from commerce. Such an interest is protected by the provisions of the treaty, and must be held inviolable under our laws. A decree of confirmation will therefore be entered in the case."

In this decision, U.S. Land Commissioner Alpheus Felch emphasized without compromise that lands acquired by the Catholic Church under the claim of use for Seminaries have been withdrawn from commercial use, and that this provision is protected by the Guadeloupe Hidalgo treaty and "must be held inviolable under our laws."

As the case was being heard in the two District courts of Northern California and Southern California, dividing this large claim in two portions, one north of Santa Barbara up to the Sonoma Mission, and including the San Rafael mission lands, the other south of Santa Barbara to the San Diego mission, the Archbishop put political pressure on a number of influential individuals, among whom the U.S. Attorney, Caleb Cushing, under the Pierce administration.

His eagerness to push his claim through the courts led him to lobby the Attorney General of the United States in order to dismiss the Congressional provisions of a mandatory U.S. Appeal, thus pursuing an unconstitutional action. After giving such an order to the two California courts on January 25, 1856, the federal administration went under a change under the newly elected President Buchanan, and Jeremiah Sullivan Black was appointed by Buchanan as new US. Attorney. One of his first actions was to revoke the order of his predecessor concerning the land claim of the Catholic Archbishop, and messages of such a reversal were sent to the two judges presiding on the case in the Northern and Southern District courts. The message reached the Los Angeles Court, allowing due process to take place, and the appeal would indeed be prosecuted in that court. In San Francisco, however, the Archbishop's case was closed before the reversal of the order reached the court. There was no Appeal as mandated by Federal law.

In the case of Marin County additional mission lands, besides the Archbishop's acquisition of the portion of Las Gallinas mission ranch through deed of Timothy Murphy, One Square League granted in 1844 by Mariano Vallejo to the San Rafael tribe was claimed by Timothy Murphy on behalf of the tribe on February 28, 1852. Timothy Murphy passed away in 1853, unaware that the claim would not be confirmed. The claim was rejected by the Commission on November 21, 1854 and dismissed for failure of prosecuting appeal on April 21, 1856. The result of this set of circumstances for the Archbishop is that all mission lands claimed by him through the U.S. Land Claim Commission north of Santa Barbara are tainted by a major flaw: unconstitutionality. This renders the title of these lands imperfect, and subject to appeal in Federal Court under the provisions of the March Laws.

The title to Mission San Rafael lands, including the deed of a portion of the Las Gallinas cattle ranch known today as the St. Vincent property, comes under this unfulfilled clause of the law. The U.S. Attorney's order to dismiss US Appeal was unconstitutional in the first place, as no Attorney General of the United States has the power to pre-empt Congressional Acts. This significant blunder taints the title of the Catholic Church to all lands acquired under the Archbishop's claim north of Santa Barbara.

The Seminary Definition

In its final decision concerning the Archbishop's Claim, the U.S. Land Claim Commission reviewed carefully the motives advanced by the Catholic Church to acquire land in California and its expressed need for such lands for "Seminaries."

The Commission redefined in clear terms what the purpose and use of those lands were, in the terms cited by Archbishop Alemany, and in a definition which clearly constitutes a ratification of the grant under the purposes brought forth by the Church as the true basis for the claim. The Decision includes the following language:

"The discipline of the Catholic Church and the decrees of the Council of Trent, which was organized as authority in Spain, imposed on the Bishop of each Diocese, the duty of establishing a Collegiate Seminary for the instruction of young men who aspire to Holy Orders. This was the origin of the Seminary for which these grants were made, and its institution and the opening of the halls of instruction was celebrated in the most formal and solemn manner by the Bishop and his ecclesiastical associates. The College was in its character ecclesiastical, and was under the general charge and superintendence of the Bishop of the Diocese; the land granted for its establishment and support was under the same charge."

The Timothy Murphy Will

On January 10, 1853, Don Timoteo Murphy took ill and convened some of his friends to redact his last will and testament at his death-bed. Witnesses to the will and deed that would shape the future of Marin County testified that his mind was clear. The friends who recorded his last wishes were his constant companion James Black, James Miller to whom Murphy had already granted a large estate, and Patrick Lambert.

These three men would become the Executors of his will. Also present were Al Barney, the local judge who lived on Murphy's land, and two men, Richards and Davis, whose testimonies under oath were taken in court after the fact.

The first order of business was the fulfillment of an ambition of Timothy Murphy, as was the fashion in those days, to grant the Catholic Church land for ecclesiastical purposes. He deeded a grant of land of 317 acres to Archbishop Alemany. The deed reads:

"Because of the desire of Timothy Murphy to make a donation to aid in the establishment of a Seminary or Institution of learning...The grantor thereby declares that the sole object of this conveyance is to establish and keep up a Seminary of learning under the care and control of the Roman Catholic Bishop, and that when said Seminary shall cease to exist, this grant is to become void and the land is to revert back to aforesaid." The language is clearly in keeping with the well-known task of the Archbishop to secure land for the establishment of Seminaries, a known fact at the time. Timothy Murphy responded to this exact stipulated need. He did not convey land for a school for girls, for an orphanage, or any other such institution. Moreover, Timothy Murphy included a "Reversionary Clause" which stipulated that if this purpose was not fulfilled, the Archbishop could not keep title to that land. There was a clear intent spelled out in the deed of the land.

The reversionary clause became subject to controversy in the following century and more recently the concern of the Church intent on eliminating it, in order to dispose of the said property without any constraint. In 1978, attorneys for the Church sought out heirs to the John Lucas line who supposedly inherited the right to recover this property at any time it was not used for ecclesiastical purposes. In their attempt to clear the title from all cloud, these attorneys furnished the Marin Court Judge with information concerning only the heirs in the John Lucas line of Timothy Murphy, leaving out all other possible heirs to the deed. These attorneys operated under the idea that the will of Timothy Murphy, co-dated with the deed to the Archbishop, specified that all such reversionary rights would be in the line of the sole inheritor of that portion of Timothy Murphy's estate. However, careful research in the State Archives has revealed that the Decree of Execution of the Will and Last Testament of Timothy Murphy contains language which clearly separates the land inheritance of John Lucas with all the rights thereof from the deed. In his Decree of Distribution of Timothy Murphy's estate, Judge Joseph Almy wrote:

"The real estate of said deceased which was heretofore distributed and delivered by said Executors Black and Miller (before their resignation) to John Lucas as devisee of said deceased, distribution is hereby affirmed and confirmed as follows: (description of the real estate ensues), excepting there from the grants **which before the date of the Will of said deceased** were made by him to James Miller and Joseph S. Alemany."

In such words, Judge Almy took the reversionary clause out of the provision of the will and left that clause securely in the deed. This means that John Lucas and his heirs have not been the sole owners of the rights of recovery of that property, a mistake the 1978 attorneys seem to have made in their representation to the court. Indeed, the deed which is by the Decree of Distribution of January 1869 the sole repository of the Reversionary Clause includes all of Timothy Murphy's heirs as holders of this right. Therefore, the 1978 effort of the Catholic Archdiocese of San Francisco to buy off this interest from the John Lucas heirs to the sum of $400,000.00, and the action taken in court on behalf of the church was incomplete and illegal. Only some of the heirs were contacted, and some of the heirs were represented to the Marin Superior Court as having all of the right to dispose of this clause, a misrepresentation of the case under the provision of the Final Decree of Distribution of Timothy Murphy's estate. The case is not closed, as the Church would like to believe, and the title to the St. Vincent's property is still clouded. Furthermore, any action on the part of one of the remaining heirs - and there are some - would reveal the illegality of the proceedings that went on in 1978.

Conclusion

This Ethnographic Report is an enquiry into the history of the properties in order to determine the cultural and historical value of the area to the people of Marin County. The report is by no means complete, and in many regards constitutes a very swift overview of certain historical eras. It provides more extensive background to its statement through the provision of additional bibliographies, archaeological and historical, which, if pursued, will provide a wealth of interesting information. The story of the Archbishop's claim and the Timothy Murphy story still need to be further elaborated.

Today, in 2013, the St Vincent property is the site of a treatment center for disturbed youth from age 7 to age 17, and is still in the hands of the Catholic Charities of the Archdiocese of San Francisco, as part of their San Francisco Peninsula-charitable programs. It is part of the Catholic Charities CYO, a nonprofit organization that provides programs and services to boys regardless of religious affiliation or socioeconomic status. The school is registered as a residential treatment center with the State of California's Department of Social Services. Currently, St. Vincent's accommodates 60 at-risk boys from abusive and troubled backgrounds. In the last few years, there has been some discussion about the use of the land for senior living facilities, and some housing development

Bibliography

1. Archeology

Cook, S. F.: "Antiquity of San Francisco Bay Shell Mounds" in: **Heizer** (1951) pp. 2022-2050.

Dietz, S. A. and Jackson, T. L.: "An Archaeological Impact Survey of the Proposed Smith Ranch development in the vicinity of Las Callinas," - Marin County, Manuscript, Laboratory of Arch Research, SF. State University.

Edwards, R. L.: "A settlement pattern hypothesis for the Coast Miwok band"- Treganza Anthropological Museum Papers, Paper No. 6 105-114.

Harding, Lawson Associates (Koh and Potter, 1987)

Kelly: 'Ethnographic Field Notes on the Coast Miwok Indians" - Ms on file at Bancroft Library, U. C. at Berkeley. (1932)

Heizer, R. F. and M. A. Whipple: "The California Indians, A Source Book" - University of California Press. (1951e)

Heizer, R. F. (Ed): "Village Names in twelve California Mission records" - University of California Arch Survey Reports, Vol. 74. (1968)

Kelly, T.: "Coast Miwok Field notes" - University of California Archives Anthropological Manuscript No. 139, Berkeley. (1932a)

Kelly, I. T.: "San Rafael Miwok Ethnography" University of California Berkeley Archives, Anthro Ms. (1932c)

King, T. F. (1970a): "Archaeological Problems and Research in the Coast Miwok area" - Treganza Museum Anthro Papers, Paper No. 6 275-288.

King, T. F. (1973b): "An Archaeological Impact Evaluation of the San Pedro Reserve near San Rafael" - Ms. - Laboratory of Arch Research -S.F. State University.

King, Thomas: - The Dead at Tiburon. (1970)

King Thomas – "The Dead Revisited" Archaeological Society Occasional Papers No. 2.

King, Thomas F. and Moratto, M. J.: "Recommended Procedures for Arch Impact Evaluation" - Society for Ca. Arch and UCLA. (1973)

King, Moratto and Leonard (1973) 5-7742, David Chavez (1985)

Moratto, Michael J.: California Archaeology Academic Press (1984)

Moratto, Michael, J.: "Anthropological Sources for San Francisco Bay," Stanford Green Library.

Nelson, N. A. "San Francisco Bay Shell Mounds "In Heizer (1951) pp. 144-157

Slaymaker Charles: "**Mrn**-138, The Material Culture of Cotomko'tca." (1977)

Treffinger, Walz and MacLeod, Planners, San Rafael (1987 Letter)

2. History

The American Indian Quarterly Special Issue: The California Indians, Vol. XIIL No. 4, U. C. Berkeley (Fall 1989)

Alley, Bowen and Co. Publishers: "History of Marin County "(1880) Bancroft Library, Berkeley.

Beals, Ralph and Joseph A. Hester, Jr: "California Indians" (1974)

Berham, Alan F. (Ms) Bancroft Library (1967)

Bingham, Helen: "In Tamal Land "(1926)

Broadstreet, Sylvia: "Studies in California Linguistics "(1964)

Chapman, Charles E.: The History of California, the Spanish Period (1939)

City of San Rafael, St. Vincent's/Silveira Advisory Committee Constraints Report Community Marin, Our future, Our Choice, A Summary of Marin Environmentalists' Recommendations for the Countywide Plan revision, May 1991.

Crevelli, J. P. (1959) Four Hundred Years of Indian Affairs in Northern Bay Counties of California, M. A. thesis, U. of Cal., Berkeley,

Diseno - Maps and Land Case Maps, Bancroft Library, Berkeley. Diseno - Map of Grant Confirmation, Rancho San Pedro, Santa Margarita y Las Gallinas, 1859 Map.

Donnelly, Florence, Independent Journal of Marin, Reminiscences of Charles Lauff (Jan 25 - May 23, 1916), (Feb 26, 1966, July 10, 1971, Jan 22, 1972)

Draft General Plan Amendment Proposal, St. Vincent's/Silveira Advisory Committee, March 25, 1994. City of San Rafael.

Garner, Van H.: "The Broken Ring," Westernlore Press, (1982)

Gibbs, George in Schoolcraft, Henry Rowe: "Archives of Aboriginal Knowledge", 3, 100-102

Hitzell, Theodore H: "History of California "(1885)

Hussey, John A.: "Mission San Rafael Archangel," - Manuscript, Bancroft Library, U. C. Berkeley

Keegan, Frank L.: "San Rafael, An Illustrated History "(1987)

Lauff, Charles A. Reminiscences, January 25 – May 23, 1916, San Rafael Independent, Anne T. Kent California Room, Marin County Library, and Marin History Museum. Photo of Ross Landing (Kentfield, early 1870's) in Kent California Room.

Little, Lucretia: "Historic Chronology of Olompali," Proposal, National Historic Register (1972)

Mason, Jack Early Marin North Shore Books (1971)

Mulet, Charles 0. (1542-1900) Chronological History of Marin County, Volumes land II (Special Collection, California Room, Marin County Civic Center Library)

Munro-Frazer, J. P.: "History of Marin County" (1880)

Murphy, Timothy - Last Will and Testament, California State Archives, Roseville

Murphy, Timothy, Estate - Probate Records, California State Archives, Roseville.

Quigley, Hugh: "The Irish Race in California," San Francisco (1978)

Quinn, Arthur: "Broken Shore, The Marin Peninsula in California History," Redwood Press (1981)

Rawls, James J.: "Indians of California, The Changing Image," University of Oklahoma Press (1984)

Reeve, Stephen, consultant, Marin Conservation League, "The Potential for Intensive Agriculture at St. Vincent's/Silveira, "no date.

Richardson, Steve: "Narrative. The Days of the Don "(1918), Manuscript.

Robinson, William: "Land in California, The Story of Mission Lands, Ranchos, Squatters."

Roop, William, Archaeological Resource Service, "A Cultural Resource Evaluation of the St. Vincent's and Silveira Properties," San Rafael, Marin County, California, June 3, 1992, A.R.S. PROJECT 92-21

Rousselin, Michel: "125 years of Marin History "(1990)

General Vallejo, Mariano - Guide to Vallejo's Documents (1780-1871), Stanford Library Rare Books.

Vallejo, Mariano - Correspondence - Microfilms, Bancroft Library, Berkeley

Vaz, August: "The Northern Missions," unpublished Ms., U. C. Berkeley - **Weber, Francis J. Mgr.:** "The Penultimate Mission: A Documentary History of San Rafael Archangel, "Libra Press United, Hong Kong.

Carmel Mission
Photo by Jennifer Hagan (2019)

The People of Niram

The Coastal Post – July, 1998

I started fieldwork among the Nacirema People a long time ago. After taking a few years off to return to my own country, visit my relatives, or visit kindred nations living in Indian Country, I began research in Niram County. The people of Niram County are very isolated from the rest of the world and provided an ideal context for anthropological research known classically as ethnography of a small community. It is difficult to find such isolated groups nowadays, as the global Nacirema civilization is engulfing the whole world. The Niram people are a specific group of Nacirema, and provided both an excellent opportunity for the understanding of a small community and the wider context of Nacirema belief, ritual and customs.

Habitat

The Niram County is a recently-developed area, inhabited by Nacirema for a very short time, about 170 years in Nacirema time. This land is situated between a bay and the ocean with an original abundance of plants, animals and people who were quickly decimated and replaced by Nacirema transplants. What remains of original life is called "wild life" and "endangered species," and is studied through rituals.

Today, the land is partitioned into three corridors, a coastal corridor reserved for wildlife rituals and recreation, with some pockets of Nacirema animals enslaved for food; the central land is mainly reserved for food production and is badly eroded and defaced. The eastern urban corridor is more intensely polluted and exploited and is carefully divided and subdivided into smaller portions, or atomized. The bulk of Niram people live in crowded lodgings in the eastern corridor, together with a few additional individuals of other origins who are restricted to foul pockets such as The Canal District and Niram City on the edges of the Niram urban world.

The myth of an original population which lived differently without cattle, roads, or permanent homes, and without an understanding of land-ownership and profits, survives dimly in the annals of Niram County. Those were the Kowim people of yore. There are small reminders of their existence in Seyer Point and a place called Otavon Museum.

Political organization

The Niram people, like all Nacirema, are organized in a hierarchical fashion as an oligarchy. Rule of Niram is mainly by age, color of skin and gender. There are some exceptions to the main rule.

Some people who do not belong to the Nacirema stock are also taken into the territory for manual labor and lowly jobs. Some darker ones are relegated in separate areas which the Niram people view as dangerous, the Niram City area, for instance, where even the conductors of mechanized chariots do not go anymore, day or night. The crime rate is too high.

Niram people view themselves as disciplined, well-regulated and compassionate people with high ethics. They take care of their needs, manage their lands judiciously, and plan for their future reasonably.

An observer coming from outside finds the Niram people to be cordial, considerate and pleasant hosts and hostesses, who are seldom curious about the origins of others. They rarely inquire if those outsiders have feelings or thought which may differ. Would they differ, they would be considered irrelevant. In general, everyone is thought to have the same values, just because they speak the same language. Even mistakes in Nacirema language are tolerated by the inhabitants of Niram, with smiles of knowing and understanding. One thing, however, which is not tolerated, is the importation of strange ideas or concepts from elsewhere. They suggest that such political turbulence would infringe upon Niram behavior and precepts, and breach the propriety of Niram existence as planned.

Cosmology

The most remarkable feature of Niram existence is their preoccupation with a god called Time, manifest in its sequences known as months, weeks, days, hours, minutes and seconds, and embodied in fetishes called clocks. Clocks are sacred objects depicting aspects of Kcolc, the Spirit of Niram land and Nacirema universe.

Clocks are arbitrary mechanisms which divide the continuous flow of daylight and night into segments. Because the Niram people like fractions and fractures, divide and count continuously, they even divided their divinity Kcolc into an infinity of little and big objects, just as they divide their other god, Ecaps, into smaller and smaller divisions they all want to own, parcels of Ecaps. While divisions of the god Kcolc is recorded in clocks, divisions of god Ecaps are kept in records called Maps, or Spam.

The Niram people seem to have both fear and respect of the ubiquitous presence of Kcolc. Every action is regulated according to its dictates and Niram people are meticulous in all their rituals to observe the demands of that god. They are in fact obsessed with ritual. The day is divided into segments ordered by Kcolc, and all life maintained by ritual.

Beliefs and mythical concepts

The central and most important objects of cult are the many replicas of Kcolc. They have different names derivative of the central divinity Kcolc. They are shaped in a variety of cloned objects of various shapes and dimensions too numerous to itemize in this short ethnography. Those are displayed everywhere, in homes, places of work and places of leisure, on their roads, inside and outside buildings. They are displayed on tables and walls, inserted in machines of transport and entertainment. Some are worn as jewelry on the wrists or as pendants and lockets. Those are called Sehctaw, or fetishes generally classified as Watch.

Each of those representations of Kcolc works in a synchronized fashioned to attune all Niram to the same spirit of Kcolc. There are penalties for not observing the imperatives of Kcolc. Nirema can miss out on tremendous opportunities if they do not obey the rules of Kcolc.

To the outsiders who know not this Kcolc or do not move to the imperatives of Kcolc, the universe of Niram may appear very bewildering and confusing. But to the Niram, those outsiders are seen as confused and possibly living outside a civilized universe. Their actions do not fuse or fit exactly with the actions of other Niram. The ideal behavior in Niram territory, as in most of Nacirema territory, is therefore perceived as Kcolc-wise or Kcolc-deprived, or non-Kcolc.

Non-Kcolc behavior is reprehensible among Niram because it is seen as uninitiated and unproductive, immature and foolish. They honor and reward Kcolced knowledge and punish or ignore non-Kcolced knowledge. Long-term research of Niram myth and ritual is by force a collage of thousands of morselled moments of Kcolc known as History.

This history is recorded in Kcolc archives and also transposed into another dimension or aspect of Kcolc on strange morselled documents containing a variety of lines and measurements. I already mentioned this aspect of the cult preserved in Maps, the SPAM cult of cartography.

Ritual

The Niram people, like all Nacirema, love ritual and cannot conceive of a single moment of their lives without ritual. Ritual, as all anthropologists have come to recognize, is a model of acceptable behavior in a community. Niram ritual can be encoded in a single day's activities. A whole ethnography of its many phases would take us very far and might be forthcoming in a future study to be entitled "Cycle of ritual among the Niram."

The one day ritual starts in all homes with sounds of Kcolc awaking the people. Sometimes, the Niram people call each other on wired ritualistic objects, the names of which mean far-sound, to remind each other it is imperative to join in the ritual of the day, and meet at the certain Kcolc moment in a parking lot, on a marsh, or a park. Others just meet at a place of work.

From that moment, every activity is strictly over-viewed by Kcolc ritual specialists who are elders or initiates in the cult. They are specially appointed for their organization and knowledge of Kcolc practices. They hand out a script encoded with notations of kcolcs-numbers, such as 10:15, 12:30 or 2:00. These numbers are accompanied by another notation which is binary: either A.M. or P.M. It is believed among these people that the day is divisible at one point called Meridian. Everything that happens before this point is called before Meridian. Everything else is after Meridian.

For further confusion of the non-initiates, the initials used for this code are borrowed from another ancient language no longer spoken in Niram County or Nacirema land: Ante Meridian and Post Meridian. There is no clear explanation for the strange mixture of languages in expressions which are either coded in the ancient language altogether, nor in a modern language understood by all.

All actions of the group are overseen by the ritual experts of Kcolc, who distribute or apportion the activities in portions of Kcolc. If one of the participants goes over his portion of Kcolc, he or she is reminded by ritual experts that it is not proper behavior. If a participant or trainee in this ritual speaks out of turn and reminds one of the ritual experts of Kcolc infraction, this is not considered proper behavior. It is simply ignored or judged as coarse, uninitiated behavior. Only ritual experts are the manipulators of Kcolc knowledge and initiative trainees in the best uses of Kcolc.

The ritual contains a series of steps over seasons or units of measurement, at the end of which the initiates declare the trainees capable of receiving the rewards and values of Kcolc sacred universe. They are formerly called "Initiates of the Society."

Conclusion

The penalty for non-observance of Kcolc Law is to be doomed to non-historical status. The non-initiates are not killed savagely, but simply relegated to the marginal status of Niram society. Marginal individuals are seen as slaves or in some cases "wild." They are kept in preserves of endangered species and other wild habitats and are slowly disappearing in a society which does not even record them on their maps.

In the case of human beings, non-Kcolc behavior is unthinkable. It is suspiciously regarded and classified as poets, artists, criminals, retarded or crazy. Criminals are easier to deal with for they are put into guarded environments strictly regulated by ways of Kcolc under guards, and by force, these people are re-educated into the good observance of Kcolc production through simple manual tasks of value to the Nacirema society, such as plates with numbers on them. The others are humored along as poets and artists of little value for Kcolc people.

Wild species and human non-initiates of Kcolc are all endangered species. They are pitied and put on certain lists which need to be managed by more knowing Kcolc people who are called "stewards" of Kcolc, instead of being appreciated for their natural wisdom as "elders."

The Kcolc people have forgotten true wisdom, and think their ritually ordained Kcolc universe is the only one that matters. Though newly installed on their lands, they have only their Kcolc ways to measure everything. They don't know that, not far from where they live, in Ksa/Iktomi Country, for instance, in the interior of Nacirema land, there are people who know of Kcolc worship, but have different beliefs which are based on non-Kcolc measurement, wit and humor, and compassionate ways unknown to Kcolc Ritual Worshippers. These people call themselves Kola or similar other names meaning friends, and they sometimes communicate in far sounds without wires and without fetishes of Kcolc and without SPAM. The Kola people know rhythms and vibrations and communicate mostly through feeling waves and dreams.

Apuleius of Madaurus

Amazigh Philosopher and World Advocate
(c. 124 - c. 180 AD)

Apuleius of Madaurus

Lucius Apuleius is known as the author of several prose masterpieces written in Latin. Apuleius of Madaurus wrote in the language of the Roman conquerors of North Africa. However, Apuleius was not a Roman. He was a native of North Africa and proud of it. Little has been made of his "Berber" origins, and the fact that he was not Roman by birth. Apuleius was strictly a citizen of Rome due to the fact that his ancestral land was then a Roman colony, and Roman citizenship had been granted to the inhabitants of the colony of Madaurus.

Apuleius is best remembered for his brilliant novel, the *Metamorphoses*, also known as *The Golden Ass*. He is the author of *Florida* and of three philosophical treatises, entitled *De Plato, De Socrates,* and *De Mundi.* In addition, a great deal of recent scholarship has paid close attention to another of his works, *Apologia* (Defense,) a unique document in the Latin classics. It is a piece of linguistic virtuosity, thought to have been orally delivered by Apuleius in his own defense in front of pro-consul Claudius Maximus and a court of Roman magistrates convened in Sabratha, a North African city not far from Tripoli. He stood accused of sorcery, an offense punishable by death under Roman law enacted in the first century.

He was indeed a "Barbarian," as he presented himself in this extraordinary speech he gave during the trial held in 158 AD. He delivered a piece of oratory so remarkable that it was circulated in print after the trial and, fortunately for posterity, was preserved in its entirety. What subsequent scholarship has failed to emphasize, however, is that Lucius Apuleius was the first Amazigh philosopher and novelist of world fame, indeed the first African to publish outside Africa. (1) He was a "Barbarian" who demonstrated with amazing virtuosity and wit that he could speak and write Latin as well as any educated Roman, and more in tune with Greek philosophy, Platonic ideals, and ancient Egyptian wisdom than the majority of his contemporaries. While Apologia has been hailed as a linguistic tour de force, magic in and of itself, it is more than superb rhetoric: it conveys an essential message reaching all Imazighen of yesterday, today, and to-morrow.

Our first Amazigh man of letters possessed a profound knowledge of ancient Egyptian ritual lore and practices. He became an initiate of the mystery cults of Neith/Tanit (Greek Isis,) and of Auser/Azzar (Greek Osiris) and was anointed 'sacerdos" or Priest of Isis and Osiris. In addition, he relates in the final chapter (chapter 48) of his famous novel The Golden Ass, apparently written long after the trial of Sabratha, that he received a third and most unusual calling. This calling was bestowed upon him in a dream when the Great Egyptian God Auser/Azzar/Osiris appeared in his full glory to call Apuleius to a worldly function which is manifestly to be most extraordinary. The mission was that of "Advocate in Court."

Apuleius believed himself to be very fortunate to receive such a calling. This ministry was so rare indeed that only one other had ever been similarly called to it. What was to be made of this divinely bestowed office? Was it a premonition, a final word referring to his legacy, or a prophecy?

Beyond the sacerdotal functions that he already exercised, Apuleius was chosen by the Gods to fulfill a certain role in the material arena of the world. The time was nearing the close of the second century AD. Lucius is retired to an ancient palace constructed in the time of Silla (around mid-century BC), dating back some two hundred fifty years. Apuleius himself faded from the public record around 180 AD, only to be discovered in the Middle Ages and re-discovered in modern times by European scholars.

At the onset of a new millennium, North Africans who are like him the descendants and cultural heirs of Numidians and Gaetulians are in deep struggle, as a people, in the face of powerful colonizers who deny them their language and cultural identity. The message delivered by Lucius Apuleius standing on trial and asserting his origins as a Barbarian, when it is not politically correct to do so, is powerful indeed. An illustrious ancestor who raises his voice in the most eloquent manner to remind us not only of his sentiment of pride in his origins but also of transcendent forces at work empowers us. He has become a true "Advocate in Court" for a whole people. I suggest that it is incumbent upon all Imazighen to re-instate him in his true place, as the first Amazigh poet, philosopher, sage, and North African literary figure to have come to world attention through his erudition, wit, and psychological and spiritual understanding of human nature.

For the most part, the ending message of Apuleius has been ignored by successive scholars. I wonder if the few laconic remarks that conclude The Golden Ass predict that his destiny was not to be weighed in terms of years but in terms of centuries, and that he had a role to play in the mundane arena of world affairs, according to a timetable of the ancient gods, and not a human timetable. Nearly two thousand years after Apuleius appeared in front of a Roman pro-consul to defend himself, playing his own "Advocate in Court," as a self- declared and proud "Barbarian," a native son of Numidia and Gaetulia, the extraordinary life of this Numidian emerges anew from scholarly archives where his real identity was ignored (however, cf. Note 2) to shine as a call to consciousness and a bright beacon.

As a scholar erudite in both Roman and Greek literatures, and a remarkable novelist and philosopher, he has of course already acquired a sort of immortality. However, the extraordinary message that he left is particularly and most meaningful to a whole group of North African people, Imazighen of today, and the future, as he takes his legitimate place in international consciousness among notable scholars and men of letters of North Africa. He is to be identified and duly honored as the forerunner of a long line of creative Amazigh sons and daughters of Numidia and Gaetulia, long denied their linguistic rights in North Africa. As such, he at last would emerge as "Advocate in Court" for all Imazighen whose culture has been labeled "oral," who have been denied a written legacy and too often been represented as Barbarians without literature. He is the very proof of the contrary. In 158 AD, this proud and immensely witty Amazigh brother made mincemeat of his accusers who were pointing to his Barbarian origins, in an exercise of linguistic virtuosity and Greco-Roman erudition unrivaled in the literary annals of the Roman world.

In my estimate, Apuleius is not only the remarkable scholar, great novelist, and spiritual figure of weight that is already recognized, but indeed an Amazigh prophet of some sort. I believe that the last vision in which Osiris appeared to him in full form and called him to his destiny as "Advocate in Court" was indeed anointing him with a special worldly task, and that his words, encapsulated in the Apologia he so masterfully delivered, were prophetic. His fame has endured through nearly two thousand years of scholarly tribute and has been particularly significant for those increasingly interested in ancient mysteries and mysticism. He must be also be re-claimed by the Numidian and Gaetulian descendants of North Africa as their first literary figure in the world court of international human rights, the world court of international consciousness. Somehow, he set the stage for this stance in his own words: "I am a Numidian and a Gaetulian, and I am proud of it. I don't see why I should be ashamed of this."

Apuleius was born around 124 AD in Madaurus, a Roman colony in the south of Numidia, which was situated in an area now located near modern Mdaourouch in Algeria, and he died some time after 180 AD in or around Carthage. He referred to this colony as a "most splendid one," ("splendissima colonia sumus," Apologia, chapter 24.) In his marvelously witty Apology, he actually spends some time describing his exact background, and his pride in it. He was, he said, both Numidian and Gaetulian. Noting the fact that he is in the eyes of his accusers a "Barbarian," he boasts of his ability to speak Latin and Greek with eloquence and practically mocks them for criticizing at the same time his Barbarian origins and his Greek oratory skills ("eloquentiam Graecam, patriam barbaram.")

It is evident from the text that Apuleius stood deliberately in front of his accusers as a native of North Africa and asserted his Barbarian heritage proudly. Though Sabratha was not yet a colony at the time of his trial, he points out the fact that his father had already served as an official of the Roman colony of Madaurus, and that his family had a certain status in that area. None the less, he is quite clear in not identifying himself as Roman. He had by then traveled the world, mastered Greek and Latin, and even taught Rhetoric in Rome before returning to his homeland in North Africa. He was familiar with Homer, Plato, and Virgil. Yet, it is his very native heritage that he stresses, while demonstrating the width and breadth of his erudition in a masterly oration, which mocks those who denigrate his origins.

At the time of the trial, the record shows that he had already undergone initiation in ancient rites and become a priest of the Great goddess of Africa and Egypt, Neith, known as Isis to the Greeks. Her ancient worship was known in archaic pre-pharaonic times in the western Delta of the Nile, and was later maintained in the numerous temples erected in her honor throughout North Africa. Apuleius was extremely interested in archaic occult knowledge from Egypt, and became an initiate of the Auser/Azziri (Greek Osiris) cult. He was also an expert herbalist, and it is believed that he wrote an entire treatise on the herbal cure of diseases, which was still in use in the Middle Ages. (2)

Perhaps it is because he was a priest of an archaic North African cult with knowledge of medicinal plants and herbs that he was perceived by the Roman authorities as a dangerous: "magician." He was responding to accusations and serious charges of having obtained through magic means an older wealthy widow's consent to marry him. He apparently successfully defended himself, and it appears that charges were dismissed following the trial.

Here is a partial quote of the passage about his origins from chapters 24 and 25 of the speech addressed to the Roman pro-consul Claudius Maximus, Semelianus, and a panel of magistrates in Sabratha:

"About my homeland, it is situated on the border of Numidia and Gaetulia. I am part Numidian and part Gaetulian. I don't see why I should be ashamed of this...

And I don't say this out of shame for my country. For even though we were once in a city belonging to the King Scyfax, when he was overthrown, we were given as a gift of the Roman people to the King Massinissa, and now, with the recent arrival of resettled veteran soldiers, we have become a most magnificent colony...

Why did I offer this information? So that from now on, Semelianus, you may be less offended by me, and so that you may extend your good-will and forgiveness, if by some negligence, I did not select your Attic Zarat as my birthplace."

The self-presentation is a seasoned mixture of indigenous pride, and unquestionable allegiance to Roman rule to the point of boast about the colony of Madaurus. It was surely dictated by the circumstances since he was on trial under serious charges possibly leading to punishment by death. His sharp wit seems also to have diluted the punches he dealt one after another.

The rich humor displayed throughout the famous speech and the depth of his initiate knowledge are particularly manifest in the work that immortalized him, The Golden Ass. More than any other part of his life works, this monumental novel has created scholarly interest and commentaries. It includes the famous tale of Psyche and Amor, as an intercalated text. This brilliant, witty, erudite, and irreverent novel is a tale of ludicrous adventures, in which the author is also the main character. It is a precursor to a literary genre in which Rabelais, Voltaire, Swift, the Picaresque novel of Tom Jones and many other followers excelled. The Golden Ass has been translated into numerous languages, used by later imitators, and has also been the inspiration and source of numerous literary works over the centuries including The Decameron, Don Quixote, and Gil Blas.

The central story of Lucius turned into an ass in search of human consciousness, and return to human form ends with a hymn to the feminine powers of the world. It is a journey which transcends time and place and offers extraordinary material for ages to come, with a modernity which has never faded. Modern day psychologists have poured over the very story of Psyche and Cupid for guidelines to journeys of transformation. They have valued the transformative powers necessary to achieve manhood alongside the mystical path offered by ancient Egyptian rites of initiation with which Lucius Apuleius was intimately familiar. His famous hymn to the Great Feminine Goddess (chapter 47) beginning with the invocation: "O blessed queen of Heaven" is still unequaled in its haunting beauty and majesty. The Supreme Goddess replies:

"Behold, Lucius, I have arrived. Thy weeping and prayers have moved me to succor thee. I am she that is the natural mother of all things, the Mistress and Governess of all the Elements, the initial Progenitrix of all things, the Chief of powers divine, Queen of Heaven, the First of the Gods celestial, the light of the Goddesses. At my will, the planets of the air, the wholesome winds of the Seas, and the silences of hell are disposed; my name, my divinity is adored throughout the entire world in various manners, in various customs and in many names, for the Phrygians call me the Mother of the Gods... Behold I am come to take pity of thy misfortune and tribulation, behold I am present to favor and aid thee, leave off thy weeping and lamentation, put away thy sorrow, for behold the healthful day which is ordained by my providence."

In the last two chapters (47 and 48), the picaresque and bawdy turn into a contrasting seriousness of tone. The catharsis is over. It has been said of Apuleius that he used his great sense of humor as a form of therapy for the soul, and that laughter and consciousness are the twin motors of the path to understanding. The great allegory is perhaps the one our people, the descendants of Numidians and Gaetulians, have traversed over the centuries, a great gale of laughter punctuating a recurring search for identity through various avatars of foreign occupation, eager to find our human countenance and full identity. This prophet of a kind shows the path. Look within, he tells us, and look at the great feminine powers of the earth, the African nature, the ancient Egyptian wisdom which is also ours, and you will become the Senators of your own ancient land and palace, this magnificent land that North Africa is. He has become for us The Senator. It is interesting to note that Apuleius uses the image of the mirror over and over. He also uses the word "viator" (nine times, it is said, and probably more) in the Golden Ass, a word that literally signified "a journeyer or traveler" but has been translated by scholars as "a free human being". His message, transcending the ages, is that he saw himself not only as a "sacerdos" (priest), but a "viator" (Amazigh, free human being.) and this message should not be lost on us. Our Senator Lucius Apuleius, nearly two thousand years ago, already embedded in the message he left for posterity the image of a free human being, "viator", or Amazigh.

In the last and forty-eighth chapter of The Golden Ass, Lucius relates how he moved from the initiation to the Mystery of the Goddess to the initiation in the archaic mystery cult of Anzar/Osiris and entered the priesthood. As a Priest of these occult mysteries, he has gained the sacred wisdom imparted by both masculine and feminine initiations, and we learn from him that the two Mysteries "unite and concord" but follow a "difference of order and ceremony." Having achieved the most profound knowledge of mystical experiences, Lucius is finally called to his extraordinary mission:

"The great God Osiris appeared to me in the night, not disguised in any other form, but in his own essence, commanding me that I should be an Advocate in the Court, and not fear the slander and envy of ill persons, which bear me grudge by reason of my doctrine, which I had begotten by much labor. Moreover, he would not that I should be any longer of the number of his Priests, but he allotted me to be one of the Decurions and Senators and he appointed me a place within the Ancient Palace which was erected in the time of Silla, where I executed my office in great joy with a shaven crown."

Is the end to the adventures of Lucius a prosaic one? No: Decurions were a specific type of Senators in the world of Roman politics. This was the name of Senators for Roman colonies, generally of native stock. It is the third movement of the great symphony of his life, where mysticism makes a leap into leadership and politics. The Palace in which he was to execute his office as a Senator was built in the time of Silla that is around 50-60 BC, and must have represented a different era, an earlier time at which the ancient Carthage had not yet been destroyed and rebuilt by the Romans. (3)

I cannot help but feel that the specific choice of this ancient palace built in the age of Silla as a place awaiting the destiny appointed to him by the gods is most interesting. A time element is clearly inserted here, as a link from the pre-Roman past to the post-Roman future. Since Apuleius saw himself truly as a "Platonic philosopher" in the Greek tradition, and his doctrine was one radically different from that of the Romans in power, he was a man of the world who had achieved a transcendent vision based on archaic powers. It is not hard to imagine that he was selected by divine interference to discharge a special office of broad import. We know that Apuleius himself spent the latter part of his life in Carthage. He left no visible trace after 180 AD, but he left us his message of transcendence. In the palace of Ancient Wisdom, he tells us in his parting prophetic words, he will have "executed (his) office in great joy with a shaven crown."

Apuleius formally conjured up Lady Philosophy to stand by his side as co-defendant in the trial that he underwent. He gave us the mirror to look at ourselves, and the great bawdy laughter to become conscious of our identity, as well as the brave words that said clearly in the face of the ruling invaders: "It is true I am not a Roman, and you call me a Barbarian. Yes, I am a Barbarian, and say I have no shame in my origins. Moreover, I can use your own language so well, so proficiently, and with such virtuosity as to make you look ridiculous in your charges of barbarism. The tools of consciousness are my own, delivered in words from your language that I throw back at you with such ease and dexterity, and the mirror image that I am placing before you is that of the other you despise through ignorance. In this defense of my identity, I am aided by all the powers of the earth, ancient wisdom, our African heritage, all the powers of transformation and true knowledge. We are the heirs to ancient Egyptian wisdom, to the Isis/Osiris mysteries of ancestral truth, to the transcendental consciousness that will outlive and outwit the centuries, and this message, I know, by the grace bestowed upon me by my dreams, will live on and become my long lived legacy as a North African philosopher and not a Roman, even though I use your language to send the message off."

It is an honor and privilege indeed to offer this late salute to the memory of such a great man as Apuleius, Amazigh prophet and "viator," for his enduring magic, his superb gift of wit and irony, and his legacy of ancient wisdom.

Notes:

1. Terentius, dramatist of an earlier era (c. 185-159 BC), was a native of North Africa. It is not clear, however, what his ancestry was, whether Roman, Punic or Libyco-Phoenician. Another North African writer, Tertullian, (c.160-225 AD) was born of native parentage. He became an outstanding lawyer. Converted to Christianity, he devoted his life and education to the defense of his Christian faith. As for Augustine, see below, note 2.

2. In the fifth century AD, Augustine, another native of North Africa was still concerned with the type of pagan beliefs espoused by the followers of Apuleius. There is evidence that towards the end of the third century AD there developed a legend around Apuleius

and his reputation for magic and supernatural powers, which pagan advocates opposed to the miracles of Christ. (Lactantius, Divin, Inst., V.3.7) The reputation of Apuleius continued to develop in the fourth century AD into the fifth, and St. Augustine felt it necessary to mention his opposition to it. (De Civ. De. VIII, 19-22-23 and Ep. 138-18.) It is noted herein that a treatise on herbal cures attributed to Apuleius was still in use in the Middle Ages.

3.   Between 60 and 46 BC, during the reign of Juba I, the North African Kingdom of Numidia is not under the rule of Romans. Juba was defeated at Thapsus in 46 BC by Caesar. The Romans officially annexed Numidia at that date and renamed it "Africa Nova." Bocchus II willed the Kingdom of Mauretania to Octavian in 33 BC. However, Mauretania was not similarly annexed by the Romans until 40 AD. It is also to be noted that the name of Mauri was applied to all non-romanized natives of North Africa still ruled by their own chiefs, until the third century AD. (Carthage, Rome and the Berbers, J.A. Ilevbare, Ibadan University Press, 1980.)

Bibliography:

Andreas, Johannes - Collected Works of Apuleius (1469) and **Apuleius** – Metamorphoses, Apologia and Florida - **Apuleius** - Philosophical Treatises - "On Plato and his Teachings." "On the God of Socrates" and "On the World."

C.S. Lewis - Till we have Faces, A Myth Retold. (1956) (Amor and Psyche)

Schlam, Carl C. - Metamorphoses of Apuleius: On making an Ass of Oneself. Chapel Hill, University of Carolina Press, 1992.

Von Franz, Marie-Louise -Psychological Interpretation of The Golden Ass of Apuleius – Out of print. C.J. Jung Institute, Zurich.

Von Franz, Marie-Louise - The Golden Ass of Apuleius, The liberation of the Feminine in Man, Jungian Studies, 1992.

Winkler, John J. - Auctor and Actor: a reading of Apuleius' Golden Ass. Berkeley University Press 1985.

A Field of Golden Mummies

Politics, Scientific Integrity and Egyptian Archaeology

The Amazigh Voice, Volume 2 and 3, No. 8 and 9, Spring/Summer 1999

Is the recently excavated giant burial ground of the Bahariya Oasis, or Field of Golden Mummies, labeled an "Egyptian" archaeological treasure, a unique and remarkable Amazigh (Berber) tribal cemetery?

The recent discovery and excavation of hundreds of mummies in the Bahariya Oasis of the Western Desert of Egypt has attracted worldwide attention. The find is extraordinary, rich beyond precedent in four types of mummies, pottery and artifacts. What makes it more valuable than any prior archaeological find in Egypt is that the site has remained intact over centuries, buried in the sand of the western desert. As a result, the burials have escaped the type of pillage and robbery to which other tombs of the Delta and Nile River were subjected before they became the objects of scientific study and international scrutiny.

On August 15, at the Natural History Museum of the City of Los Angeles, a symposium, held by the Southern California Branch of the American Research Center in Egypt, featured two archaeologists who are very much in the news. On that day, an audience of about two hundred "Egyptologists" was entertained with the fabricated notion that Cleopatra was a Barbarian Queen.

The first guest was Dr. Zahi Hawass, Director of the Sakkara and Giza Pyramid sites, member of the Egyptian Supreme Council for Antiquities, and newly appointed to the position of Under Secretary of State for Giza, and Sakkara. The focus of his presentation was the latest excavations in the Oasis of Bahariya, which he had directed. A slide show accompanied his presentation.

The second guest was Dr. Jean Yves Empereur, also recently in the news for his Salvage Archaeology of the harbor of Alexandria. He is Director of Research of the Center for Alexandrian Studies and a Research Director for the National Center for Scientific Research of France. At the opening, Dr. Allison Futrell, a Professor of History at the University of Arizona, who has just completed a forthcoming book entitled "Barbarian Queens", provided a historical context for the archaeological findings.

First, history indicates that in about 600 BC, Alexander the Great conquered and colonized North Africa and implanted a Greek lineage of kings and queens which eventually produced Cleopatra. The Greek identity of the Queen of the Nile is evident from her portraits on coins of the era. That said, one would never have known, from Dr. Futrell's presentation, that Cleopatra was anything but Egyptian, a Ptolemaic Queen who identified herself with Isis. Not once did Dr. Futrell discuss

Cleopatra and Alexander in the light of a conquered Egypt, with its indigenous population of "Barbarians." Cleopatra, like other Greeks, no doubt despised the very Egyptian population of "Barbarians" (Libyans in the west, Nubians and Sudanese in the South) with which this latest American historian identified her.

Scheduled for publication this fall, Dr. Futrell's forthcoming book on Cleopatra and other "Barbarian Queens" has the potential to introduce yet another distortion of the history of the North African people. The term "Barbaroi" was used by the Greeks to refer to the Libyans. Consequently, to represent Cleopatra as a "Barbarian Queen" is a distortion of history, as Cleopatra was not Libyan, Berber or Amazigh.

Dr. Hawass traveled to the Oasis of Bahariya, located 200 kilometers west of Alexandria, and visited Siwa, the Amazigh (Berber) oasis south of Bahariya. During the narration of his journey to the two oases, Dr. Zahi Hawass did not once mention the ethnic population of this desert area, be it now or at the time the burials occurred (200 BC to 100 AD). When he mentioned the small local temple dedicated to Alexander the Great near the Oasis of Bahariya, he did state that Alexander briefly voyaged from Alexandria to the region. Surprisingly, Dr. Hawass omitted to provide the reasons and the extent of Alexander's journey. However, the historical record is clear: Alexander the Great only traversed the region of Bahariya on his way to the oasis of Siwa, because he needed to reach the source of legitimacy in Egypt, the settlement from where the first priesthood of the central God of Egypt, Amon, is said to have originated. He needed to be empowered by the Issiwann, spiritual guardians to early Egyptian religious traditions.

The Greeks called the inhabitants of the Oasis of Siwa "Ammonoi", and the locality "Ammon." The God Ammon was the equivalent to Zeus in Greek mythology or Jupiter in the Roman pantheon of Gods.

Dr. Hawass not only omitted these details, but he spoke of traveling himself to the Oasis of Siwa without indicating the reason for his interest in it. Siwa people are an Amazigh (Berber) speaking group. In fact, the whole region of this desert of Western Egypt is known to scholars for being Libyco-Berber territory.

The field of mummies found by Dr. Hawass is located near the ruins of a fort dating back to Roman occupation, which occurred after the defeat of Cleopatra and followed the Greek colonization of the area. The Greek Ptolemaic Dynasty which was inaugurated by Alexander the Great reigned in Egypt from 600 BC to 200 BC at Alexandria, and the Roman colonization in the vicinity of Alexandria lasted from that time to about 100 AD. The dating of this giant cemetery, tentatively thought to cover four square miles of desert, and possibly holding the remains of bodies, seem to span several centuries over the Greco- Roman period.

When the floor was opened to questions, I requested from Dr. Hawass additional information about the ethnicity of the people of Bahariya. Dr. Hawass said that they were "Egyptians." When I suggested that in 200 BC, in the desert west of Alexandria, the indigenous populations were Libyco-Berbers or Amazigh, like the population of the Oasis of Siwa today, Dr. Hawass was very quick to assert that he had said "Egyptians". He added that these people looked like me. He continued in haste to add that they looked like him too and that their origin was no other than Egyptian. To conclude his commentary, he indicated the following: "I know nothing about the people you mentioned."

Later, during a private conversation with him, I inquired about any documentation or historical record, Roman or other, on the existence of this Roman fort that had been erected near a substantial local population of Libyans (which he had estimated at being well into the hundreds of thousands over time). Dr. Hawass categorically denied the existence of any such records. "Nothing is known of this population in the annals of history," he essentially repeated, asserting that these mummies are of an undefined origin. He added that these mummies were of no particular ethnic origin and that there were simply Egyptians and definitely not Roman or Greek. He also mentioned that some of them appeared to be fairly wealthy, and might have been artisans or involved in a thriving wine-making community.

Dr. Empereur, in a later private conversation, corroborated my tentative hypothesis about the ethnic origin of these mummies, by saying that it is most likely that the Bahariya people were Berber or Amazigh. He also indicated that he was familiar with French linguistic research, which places populations of Berber speakers throughout Libya, the Oasis of Siwa and the whole western desert of Egypt. "It is therefore justifiable," he said, "to state that these burials are of Berber people. They most likely are." When questioned on Dr. Hawass's evasive position, Dr. Empereur readily admitted that we were talking about "Colonial Archaeology."

Indeed, such was precisely the point, and Dr. Hawass, as a scientist, had quickly evaded the issue of indigenous burials in front of an audience of two hundred people. He also publicly stated his lack of knowledge of the origins of such burials, to avoid the cultural and political repercussions that such recognition would entail. This evasion raises the question of scholarly probity, and historical truth, not to mention the rights of disposal of these sites, a political question of no small dimension.

When I shared some of my concerns with Amazigh (Berber) people through a quick internet note, Dr. Hassan Ouzzate, Associate Professor, Faculty of Letters and Humanities at Ibn Zohr University of Agadir, Morocco, provided the following comments: "...Egypt is particularly bad in this domain... Egyptian historical vestiges are there to belie such an attempt. What happens is a very selective account of truth. Official historical accounts have always considered any cultural influence coming from "west" of the Nile (The Land of the Dead) as nefarious to a mythical central Egypt... The name of the group you mentioned (Bahariya) attracted my attention as a possible Amazigh form for the following three reasons:

1. It is a collective name for the people, not a geographic name. Why? Because it is the usual Arabized plural form given to a great many tribal names throughout North Africa. Examples: Gzennaya, Schawiyya, and Ghardaya.
2. One can easily return the form to its original

Amazigh: Igzenayn,

Iccawn,   Igherdayn...

It is clear that the derivation is from "BHR" (or Arabic BHARI") meaning "of the sea"... Therefore "abehri" (Pl, ibehriyn) is a perfectly good Amazigh term, denoting the "people of the sea," whether that means "by the sea" or "from the sea" or "living off the sea". Notice that if the power of naming resided with the Siwa Oasis, an agricultural, sedentary and inland group, the appellation would be very logical."

In addition, I consulted the published research of Mohammed Chafik, member of the Moroccan Royal Academy, on the topic of the prehistoric origins of the Egyptian pyramids. His work includes specific information on the Oasis of Siwa, the travels of Alexander the Great in the area, and the common linguistic origins of Berber and Egyptian burial complexes. It is from Mohammed Chafik's work that I learned of Alexander's visit to Siwa, and became familiar with the Arabic poem that he quoted. Dr. Chafik notes that the journey of Alexander the Great to that oasis must have been of great importance to the antique world, for ten centuries after it occurred, the poet Umayya Ibn Abl es-Salt related Alexander's journey: "He (Alexander) reached the West, seeking from the Guides of Wisdom some foundations for his power. So he went, in the direction of the setting sun, where, at evening, the sun sets near a source of bubbling waters." There are well-known bubbling wells of salt water in the region, more than two hundred in the Oasis of Siwa. Dr. Chafik concluded his remarks on the ancient sanctity of this region of Amazigh culture with the following comments: "Though experts are still debating which one of the two temples of Ammon, that of Thebes or that of Siwa, was founded before the other, all indications point to the anteriority and the primacy of the oasis complex of the Libyan desert." (Tifinagh: Revue de Culture et de Civilisation Nord-Africaines, August 1997).

Images of Bahariya mummies in this essay courtesy
of photographer Kenneth Garrett.

In conclusion, it is my opinion that once again in a long series of historical misdeeds and cultural distortion, the scientific world is about to be tarnished by another form of violence to history. This violence results from the short -sightedness of Egyptian scholars and Egyptian leadership, which might be afraid to respect the truth for political reasons. In Egypt, it is more politically correct to declare all finds "Egyptians" and to refuse to discuss the ethnic origins of this find. However, it is ethically incorrect and deplorable to deny the international community the truth of history in the name of nationalism and the protection of Middle Eastern interests in Africa.

A cultural treasure is about to be plundered once again. This time, it is the case of the refusal of Egyptian scholars and the Egyptian government to address the Amazigh origin of the archaeological treasure. On that August Sunday afternoon, an entire audience of American Egyptologists was misled into thinking that the newly discovered field of Golden Mummies covering a large portion of the western desert of Egypt contains human remains of undetermined origin

Notes:

1. Dr. Hawass published a magnificent coffee table book in 2000. "Valley of the Golden Mummies" with superb photography of those mummies and artifacts found alongside of them. The book offers the very same haunting photographs that evoked such a strong response on my part.

2. By 2000, Dr. Hawass has had time to reflect on his find, and has received a copy of this article which I personally mailed to him. He confides of nightmares where mummies of children who have been separated from the mummies of their parents and grand- parents come to haunt him in his sleep and threaten to strangle him. He is led to understand the imperative need to respect the lineal descent of those children, and their genealogy, their ethnicity. He wrote the following statement on page 89 of his book, in the chapter titled "Mr. X Goes to Giza.": "In the near future, we hope to complete DNA analyses of the mummies from the Valley of The Golden Mummies to unlock the mystery of the exact genealogical ancestry of the population of Bahariya during the time the cemetery was in active use. In the same way that DNA from the mummies was used to determine the identity of the royal mummies at the Cairo Museum, it may also confirm the archaeological and historical evidence that Bahariya was inhabited by Libyans…"

Islam And The Enslavement Of Africans

I recently came across a Tikkun Magazine article featuring a former slave of Mauritania, Mr. Moctar Teyeb. The article appeared under the title of "A Call to Freedom," published in 2000. I was at the time researching the extent of the participation of Berbers to the institution of African slavery, the slave castes of the Western Sahara, Mauritania and the Tuareg groups, as well as the infamous Saharan Slave Trade of North Africa. The task assigned to me by the World Amazigh Congress, an international organization of Berbers (Imazighen) was to elucidate the topic of slavery in North Africa, and not that of exculpating or inculpating any particular group. I was to submit a report based on my findings for the United Nations Conference on Racism and Discrimination scheduled for the following year in Durban, South Africa.

Mr. Moctar Teyeb, the informer for the Tikkun Magazine article, has first- hand knowledge of an existing problem in his native country of Mauritania. However, he may not have had access to some of the extensive historical material available on the matter which could allow him to modify some of the statements he makes in his appraisal of the historical context of slavery in Africa in general and the Slave Trade more particularly. Apparently, neither did Tikkun, the publisher of his article. Otherwise, I am sure the Editor would have provided some notes for the benefit of the readers of Tikkun, as to the perhaps little known but serious participation of North African Jews to the traffic of slaves in Africa, not to speak of the necessary distinction between Arabs and Berbers, two distinctive ethnic groups, Berbers being the aboriginal people of North Africa. This important distinction was entirely omitted in this article, and no mention was made of the fact that numerous Berbers were converted to Judaism long before Islam entered their lands, and many "pagan" Berbers were themselves enslaved by Arab invaders.

The writer opened his story with this statement: "Eight centuries ago, my ancestors lived peacefully in their homeland in Africa. Then came the Arab-Berbers raids." As we enter the 21st century, this sentence places the origin of enslavement practices of Mauritania at the 12th century AD. Mr. Teyeb purposefully ignored the preceding centuries of enslavement practices in Africa by Black Africans in sub-Sahara countries, and their involvement in the Slave Trade after the arrival of Arabs and Islam. Slavery existed prior to the arrival of the Arabs in Africa in the 7th century, as an African institution. His further assertion that "as a result of those caravans, slavery began as an accepted institution in the region in which I was born," needs to be scrutinized and differentiated.

Djebel Bani, Nomad, Moroccan Pre-Sahara (Helene Hagan, 1997)

It is known that the caste system existing in that area is not so much directly related to the caravan trade as it is to the importation on an ideology – Islam – which upheld the superiority of believers over non-believers, and created the subsequent views that pagans of Africa could be enslaved with impunity. I would like to recapitulate briefly some of the important facts of this historical development.

The first people enslaved in North Africa were the indigenous Berbers (Imazighen, meaning "Free People") who were enslaved by the tens of thousands by colonizing Phoenicians to run their plantations and man the oars of their powerful fleet of ships. The Romans had a somewhat different relation to these indigenous people of Africa, while the only "black" slaves Rome might have known were not from sub-Saharan countries, but from Upper Egypt, the country known as Nubia. The records show that they were relatively few since Romans relied more originally on war captives from European campaigns, then on Jewish revolts and subsequently on slave offspring from their existing slave population. By the time they arrived in North Africa, they had enough of a supply among their slave population to meet their needs, with the majority of their slaves coming from that group, criminals and a plentiful number of orphans.

The Arabs began to invade and defeat Egypt, Libya and the Maghreb regions of North Africa from 644 AD and afterwards in successive waves of invasion until the 11th century. Who were the defeated populations? They were the various groups of indigenous Berbers. The first policy of Arabs, as clearly established by historical documentation, was to tax the inhabitants of these regions with such heavy war taxes that the sale of Berber women and children was included in their treaties with Berber groups as a means to come up with the tax. The first treaties with Libyan groups stipulated 360 women and children annually from each conquered village or group. This practice was continued throughout the invasion of North Africa, which occurred westward all the way to the Atlantic Coast, where the enslavement of women and children remained a substantial part of the booty collected by Arab conquerors and their forces.

One must remember that the Arab invaders brandished the Koran, which explicitly stated that the enslavement of non-believers was permissible. The first idea of enslavement on the part of Arabs was sanctioned by their religious ideology: only non-believers (all pagans) could be sold in slavery. The Koran pretends to a certain noble humanity by saying that once they adopt the faith of their masters and conquerors, that of Islam, the vanquished can be "redeemed" from their slave status. Mr. Moctar Teyeb underlines, and rightly so, that both masters and slaves of Mauritania are of the Islamic faith. I would add, it is because they are all believers in the same book which upholds that slavery is permissible that, today, in that region of Africa, the institution is widespread and even the Islamic courts favor it. The first sanction of slavery came from Allah. Ideology and divine authority are the pillars on which millions of human beings have been "justifiably" enslaved.

Soon, the steady supply of Berber women and children from Libya, Tunisia, Algeria and Morocco, collected for the needs of the wealthy emirs by then settled in Egypt, as well as those of Arabia, became inadequate, and even Islamicized Berbers became the target of Arab slavers. History reveals the number of slaves extracted by certain leaders of the conquest and occupation of North Africa. Among them, I have retained the documented figures of 315,000 for one and 400,000.00 for another of those invading lords of Arabia. The Arab essayists who reported those figures might have exaggerated somewhat, but nonetheless, the number of slaves coming from North Africa was substantial. This took place in North Africa between the seventh and ninth centuries, with numerous rebellions of Berber groups during those centuries. Until the crucial expedition of 734 AD, the Sahara and western sub-Saharan countries were not part of the slave-oriented needs of Arab consumers. The Arab invaders of North Africa, keen on locating where the gold of the Berbers came from, organized an expedition to the Souss and south of Morocco to find the location of gold traded among Berbers. This expedition was fateful in that it created what would become the western routes of the infamous Trans-Saharan Slave Trade.

A close examination of Arab texts leads to the inevitable conclusion affirmed by scholars that this Trans-Saharan Slave Trade of Black Africans started indeed in the eighth century, with this 734 D expedition. The second powerful motive, which enters history, is then greed, and a huge commercial and financial enterprise was mounted. Berber tribes who controlled key oasis settlements of the Sahara soon learned that they could enrich themselves by this trade, and began to impose heavy taxation on any traffic through their lands, while also furnishing guides, scouts, supplies, and camels at a price. The security provided by nomadic warriors of the desert also was costly to the financiers of the slave Trade, as the Tuareg Tribes leased their policing forces at high prices and also began to profit by this trade. Let us examine, however, who actually financed, organized and directed this immensely profitable trade.

Caravans were organized and financed by Turkish bankers, Arabs, and Jewish merchants of the North. Many entrepreneurs of foreign countries, living in littoral urban settings of Cyrenaica at Tripoli, around the slave trade center of Benghazi, and in thriving port communities of Morocco, were the financial backers and final profiteers of the Slave Trade during the flourishing era of the trade. In 1591, a Moroccan expedition destroyed the Kingdom of Songhai, and in the 16th and 17th centuries, the routes of the central Sahara were dominated by Tuareg (Berber) tribes. In the 17th and 18th centuries European traders dominate the Slave Trade. After the death of two Arab slave hunters, Rabah and Samori (1900), famous for their "rezzous" on horseback, a clear decline of the Trans-Saharan traffic occurred. Great Britain, the largest slave trading state enacted Anti-Slavery laws in 1837, and France followed in 1848. The centuries old practices that had created a specific type of economy in the desert oases and the Sahara sustained a deep blow from colonization, and the character and social structures of the entire Sahara desert population were destroyed. Slavery practices and serfdom (two categories of Saharan societies) upon which castes of warriors and holy men of Berber ancestry built wealth and power became obsolete. Mauritania, on the occidental side of the Sahara, is a new post-colonial nation where, despite the existence of rich iron mines which makes it valuable to the Western corporations and states exploiting the various underground resources of Africa, traditional hierarchical societies persist in the essentially barren environment of the desert.

For centuries, huge caravans were needed to transport the goods and the slaves. To equip them, load them with supplies, and provide a safe journey through dangerous territories traversed by numerous groups of nomadic tribes, Arabs and Berbers, the moguls of the Slave Trade had to put enormous amounts of cash up front. Seed money was provided by Turkish and Jewish bankers and merchants before the arrival of European capital. The cost of providing escorts of some 300 to 400 mounted Tuaregs to protect them along the way made it also a very expensive proposition. These commercial enterprises developed not only well run departure and arrival centers with slave depots, but intermediary secure caravan stops. In these centers, they maintained relatives, non-Berber and non-black personnel, to oversee the traffic in North Africa, in sub-Saharan regions, and in the desert of the Sahara. Timbuktu was a central crossroad to four different routes toward Morocco, Algeria and Tunisia, but there were other centers.

Such was the enormous enterprise of the well-known Mardoche Brothers, five Jewish brothers, native of Akka, descendants of Spanish Jews. Their letters outline the procedures, the structure of their vast organization (with brothers at key points), the cost of caravans and the mode of transport and security needed for their dangerous travel though the desert. From these numerous letters, we have an ample record of the Black African Slave Trade from 1859 to 1879. The Jewish Mardoche brothers held the monopoly of this Trade in the Moroccan and Algerian routes, (Timbuktu/Tindouf/Djisilmassa) but they had their counterpart in the Tunisian and Libyan routes. Several top executives on record were merchants of Tripoli, Jewish for the most part, such as the one who took up the name of Hassan but was actually an Italian Jew of the large Jewish community of Livorno, or Arabs like a certain Hadj Mohammed Barbari. Market competition was high, and the better organized relied on family members located at strategic points, such as the Mardoche Brothers Enterprises.

In addition, the record shows that the Kehath family from southern Morocco settled in Timbuktu, converting to Islam in 1492. The Cohen family descending from the Moroccan Jewish trader al Hajj Abd-el-Salaam al Kuhin is recorded in Timbuktu in the 18th century, and in the 19th century, the Abana family. Furthermore, Rabbi Mordachai Abi Serour came from Morocco in 1860 to be a trader in Timbuktu.

A number of ancient manuscripts preserved in Timbuktu reflect the overseeing capacity of those Jewish traders as some of the accounting records are annotated in Hebrew characters on their margins.

The market demands of Arabia and Egypt grew enormously. At the top of its unceasing appetites for black slaves were the women mostly used for cooks and domestic need (Arabs continued to favor white slaves for sexual pleasures, though black ones were not excluded), children and young castrated males being second in demand. The casualties of castration performed by sub-Saharan African barbers on young black men of Africa have been calculated at up to 90%. It was only later that the military needs of the Sultans of Morocco (Moulay Ismail who was an Emir of Egypt with a commander of troops in Morocco was the creator of the first army) equally relied on that market to form the well-known Sudanese ranks of their army, and subsequently that of the Royal Black Guards of Morocco. While the consumers were the Arabian lords, the bankers were primarily

Turkish, and the mercantile top executives were Jews, the Berber oasis dwellers were the middle management and the Berber Tuareg warriors were the police force. The participation of black Africans in the capture and original sale transactions in sub-Saharan regions cannot be omitted from the overall business scheme. Among the Berber tribes seriously involved in the Trade were the Massufa, the Lamta, the Mazata, the Hawwara, and the Hafusa, tribes that were all defined as "Ibadite" Berbers settled on the edge of the Sahara Desert.

Ideology was the primary factor in creating a class of slaves in the Arabic world, and ideology preceded by far the enslavement of Black Africans by Arabs, when it obtained a class of slaves from the Berber Free Men of North Africa. The greed of Arab conquerors, backed by Turkish financiers and mercantile Jews, was the secondary factor and initial motive for the Trans-Saharan Slave Trade in general.

In Mauritania, Islamic ideology, and Arab conquest also brought about the social structure mentioned (but not explained) by Moctar Teyeb. He makes clear that both masters and slaves are Muslim. He also unfortunately includes the Harratin as fellow slaves, which they are not. The Harratin have mysterious origins, which scholars have long debated. They are more closely related, genetically, to the Berbers of North Africa than to Black Africans, and yet they are a black-skinned population. Some scholars have seen in them the direct descendants of the original prehistoric inhabitants of the Sahara. They once worked in the oases of the desert as serfs or domestic servants of the Tuaregs, and considered themselves closely allied to them, forming a class category, which was not equated by Arabs or Tuaregs with that of slaves. Indeed the Arabic word for slave is "Abd," a word not applied to Harratin people. At the time Moulay Ismail gathered his elite black troops (14th century,) his general El Bakhri conscripted some Harratin, to the outcry of the Scholars of Fez and of the general population of Morocco, creating a great stir in the country, as Harratin were considered to be "Free Men" or "Imazighen not subject to a conscription of black slaves.

The Arabs inculcated to the vassal Berber tribes paying war tribute to them that Arab, and white was best (numerous Berber tribes were of darker color from previous mixing of populations in the desert): therefore, genealogies were fabricated to give entire groups of Islamic Berbers Arab ancestry. Thus, Mauritania has a caste of "white" Beydanes. The Hassaya speakers of Mauritania (about one million) call their territory "trab-l-bidan" (the land of the white man) and themselves "Beidanes" ("white men.") They are the "Moors" or descendants of Sanhaja Berbers converted to Islam about 1,000 years ago and of Arab invaders who came several centuries later. Their area of dominion is opposed to the Savannah regions of the south, peopled by the black people of the grasslands ("Toucouleurs" of Peul language) whom they call "Abd," meaning slave in Arabic. Arab warrior classes and the vassal religious Berber groups with fictitious Arab lineage are contrasted to that of "black" African ancestry, originally pagan, and often seen as reverting to pagan ways in spite of being converted. This remarkable formation of structural classes and the construction of a caste system based on Arab "white" lineage took over the whole area, distorting the actual genetic and ethnic origins of certain groups of the desert. The persistent supremacist ideology of the Arabs prevailed over common sense. To have access to wealth and power, entire groups of Berbers claimed ancestry in Yemen or from the lineage of the Prophet (i.e., the Reguibat of the Western Sahara), in order to gain status and recognition.

The catastrophic message of the Koran (enslave the non-believers you conquer in the name of Islam) and the use of this message made by Islamic followers, in their assertion that Arab means white and superior to African and black, resulted in the present-day situation in the entire region. There are over thirty million Berbers and a good number of them, some in the Western Sahara and Mauritania, identify with Arabs, linguistically, religiously, and even through the invention of fictitious genealogies.

While the view of Moctar Teyeb is understandably a valuable message, as a personal testimony of a man born to slavery under local and temporal social constructs based on a specific type of ideology, his report that "Arabo-Berbers" were the agents of historical events which enslaved his people needs to be read in the light of the ample documentation which exists on the institution of slavery in Africa, and the nature of the Trans-Sahara Slave Trade. The Berbers of North Africa and the Berber Tuareg groups of the Sahara desert – all Imazighen – succumbed to the tyranny of Arab conquest, rule, and ideology, some of them to the point of creating legends and myths which gave them, the conquered, the same authority and superiority as their assailants and conquerors. While some have arabicized themselves thoroughly, in order to escape the slave status, others continue to struggle against the supremacist views of Arabs.

Finally, as regards the publication and transmittal of Moctar Teyeb's somewhat incomplete message to the readers of Tikkun, a reminder about the large contribution of North African Jewish merchants to the establishment and maintenance of a Trans-Saharan Slave Trade through the centuries, must be noted. Different sentiments emerged in the last century toward the formerly widespread institution of slavery. It was an institution which sustained a specific type of economy throughout entire Black kingdoms and the Sahara desert. Then, Africa joined the capitalist global economy and its democratic basis, and reparation is now demanded by some for the thinking of an earlier age. Then, any reparation must come from the Jews as well as from the Berbers in addition to the primary reparation from the Arabs, and must include equally all Islamic groups of Black Africa who participated in such an abusive commerce of human lives. The Arab conquerors of Africa, along with their Islamic teachers, are those who most bear the burden of responsibility for a specific mode of thinking, encoded in a religion they spread throughout the African continent, and was perpetuated in a behavior originally dictated by an exclusive God obviously alien to African spirituality.

A Brief Chronology:

5,000 BC - Pastoral economy of the Sahara Desert – Evidence of mixed populations co-existing. The Haratin black-skinned population is considered to be the direct descendants of some of the Negroid Paleolithic groups of this area, genetically and linguistically different from Black Africans of the sub-Sahara regions. The Haratin are not considered to be a slave category (Arabic "Abd"), but Free Men of dark skin. They are serfs or domestic servants of the Tuaregs and partake of their culture. In recent history, some have become wealthy owners of property in oases while Tuareg warriors, once the uncontested Lords of the desert, are no longer able to maintain traditional modes of subsistence practically annihilated by French and British colonization, and have fared poorly.

(Note: The Blue Men of Mauritania and Western Sahara are the descendants of the last Arab invaders of the 15th century, proud of their pure Arab ethnicity, by comparison with the mixed one of vassal Berbers and that of the black slaves.)

7th – 8th centuries – Era of Arab invasions, propagation of Islam and domination of Maghreb by waves of Arab invaders. Indigenous Berber groups are decimated, enslaved, converted to Islam and arabicized.

9th century – Creation of caravan routes through the Sahara, with trails from occidental Sudan (Arabic term for "Land of the Black People") to Morocco dominated by converted Berber groups in the oases, and caravan stops.

11th century – Dynasty of Saharan Berber Almohavids in the "Maghreb." The term "Maghreb" is an Arabic word which is used to designate "the land of the setting sun, the far west" evidently in relationship to the Peninsula of Arabia. It is a term erroneously adopted by Europe, when the right name for the region would be "North Africa."

12th century – Almohads, a Berber dynasty which succeeded that of the Almohavids in the "Maghreb."

14th –15th centuries – Timbuktu is the central Sahara slave depot.

1591 – A Moroccan expedition is led to the land of the blacks, to obtain gold, salt and slaves and the Kingdom of Songhai is destroyed.

16th – 17th centuries – The caravan routes and Trans-Saharan Slave Trade flourish and are dominated by the Tuareg warriors, Blue Men (Occidental Sahara warrior tribes) and Berber oases (religious brotherhoods, maraboutic rule.)

17th – 18th centuries – The European Slave Trade takes over.

1837 and 1848 – British and French pass anti-slavery laws, but slave trade persists in practice, with tacit approval of colonizers.

1894 – Senoussya (Muslim sect) exhort and back up Tuareg warriors to pillage the sedentary villages of the Sahel, and shackle their prisoners who are sold in the North for high prices.

1880-1910 – Decline of Trans-Saharan caravan routes.

Bibliographic Sources from Antiquity:

"Le Periple d' Hannou," is a text that dates from the Fifth century before Christ, with a reference to the presence of "blacks" in the Maghreb. (André Adam, Alger, 1972 – "Bibliographie de Sociologie, Ethnologie et Géographie Humaine du Maroc, p 19.)

310 BC - **"Asphodales"** of Diadorus. The presence of black Africans living in the center of present-day Tunisia is mentioned. This presence is later evaluated as being attributable to a few slaves of Carthagenian masters, of Nubian or Ethiopian origin, as relations between that region and territories south of the Sahara are not evident. (Citation page 8 in

"*Carthage, Rome et les Berbères*, J. A. Herbara, Ibadan University Press, 1980.)

420 AD - The Latin poet **Florus** mentions in pejorative terms the import of slaves furnished by Garamantes in Roman Africa, at Hadrumetum, nowadays region of the Suss in Tunisia. The quote is as follows: "Faex Garamantarum nostrum processit ad axem et piceo gaudet corpore verna niger."

Another Roman Poet, Luxorius, also noted the import into Roman Africa of female Garamantes slaves. See "Ut tibi non placeat Pontica, sed Garamas." (*Luxorius*, **43.**)

Arabic Historians, Geographers and Essayists:

(Primary sources in translation or secondary sources furnished by documents of the 19th and 20th centuries.)

Quote:

"From the region of Tagadda, West Africa, come excellent young slaves, eunuchs, and saffron-dyed cloth." Ibn Battuta, 1353.

- **Al Yaqubi,** Persian Geographer (died 889 AD) left us a list of names of groups living in Eastern Libya at the end of the 9th century in his work of "*Kitab-al-Budan,*" translation, Leiden, 1892.

- **Tadeus Lewicki** (cf. Bibliography) collected data from Arabic sources (geographers) of the 9th and 10th centuries.

- **Chronicles of Timbuktu:** Ibn Harukal (10th century,) Ibn Battuta (14th) and Leo Africanus (16th)

- **Chronicles of the Maghreb:** El Bakri (11th), Idrissi (12th) Yakub (13eme): Ibn Khaldun, Al Omari (14th.) and Al Maqrizi.

- The most exact and clearer text on the topic of the conquest of North Africa is viewed by scholars as furnished by Ubayd Allah b. Salih b. Abd al Hakam au 13th century. This text furnishes what we know of the raids of Uqba Ibn Nafi.

- The recounting of the sale of Amazigh (Berber) women from North African tribes in rebellion, in public auctions of the slave markets of Cairo, is given by **Murray Gordon**, page 30 of his work, *"Slavery in the Arab World."* (cf. Bibliography.)

- The legal opinion of **Ahmed Baba of Timbuktu** dates from 1023. It is present in several documents of Morocco. Two manuscripts exist, one in Paris, the other in Rabat, Morocco.

- **Khalil Ibn Islaq** (Tome I, page 216) has given us ample information on the type of "humiliation" which was imposed upon the indigenous peoples of North Africa.

- Seven Arabic texts mention the sale of Berber women and children by North African groups, in order to meet the war taxes imposed by the Arabic conquerors. Six of those texts were written after the 10th century. (See Arabic sources above.)

- Ample information on Jewish merchants who are famed for their eunuch factories in Andalusia during the tenth century emanate from several sources, the first source being that of Arabic Geographer **ibn Hawqal.**

- **Ibn Al Khalib** (14th century) is the source of data on the Maqqari Jewish brothers, the Mardoche family and its slavery monopoly.

- **Ibn Khaldun** (14th century) is the sole historian who has written of the devastation by the Hillalian and Sulaymite tribes throughout Ifriqya. (His work rests on preceding Arabic writers.)

Bibliography

Abitbol, Michel - Juifs Magnrébins et Commerce Trans-Saharien du VIIIème au XIVème Siècle in «Le Sol, La Parole et l'Ecrit, Mélanges en hommage à Raymond Mauny» Paris, 1981, 2 Vol.

Adam, André – *Bibliographie Critique de Sociologie, d'Ethnologie et de Géographie Humaine du Maroc.* Alger, 1972.

Arkell, A.J. – *History of the Sudan till AD 1822.* The Athlone Press, 1955.

Barrows, General, D.P. - *Berbers and Black*, 1931.

Bates, Oric – *The Eastern Libyans*, 1914.

Bovill, E.W. – *The Golden Trade of the Moors* (also titled "Caravans of the old Sahara) Oxford University Press, 1968.

Brett, Michael & Fentress, Elizabeth – *The Berbers*, Blackwell Publishers, 1997

Camps, Gabriel – *Recherches sur les cultivateurs Noirs du Sahara* – Revue de L'Occident musulman (1970.)

Camps, Gabriel – *Civilisations préhistoriques*, Paris, 1974.

Chabrolles, Michel – *Les hommes du voile*, 1990.

Chassey, Francis de – L'étrier, la houe et le Livre, "Sociétés Traditionnelles au Sahara et au Sahel Occidental," Editions Anthropos, 1977.

Chapelle, Jean – *Nomades Noirs du Sahara*, Paris, Plon, 1957.

Chater, Khalifa - "Arabic Source Material in North Africa for the Study of the trans-Sahara slave trade."

Cotton, Samuel – *Silent Terror, a Journey into contemporary African slavery*, Harlem River Press, 2000.

Daget, Serge – *La traite des Noirs* - Éditions Ouest France, 1990.

Daniels, C.M. – *The Garamantes of southern Libya*, Michigan, 1970.

De Gaid, Mouloud - "Les Berbères dans l'histoire" - Tome I, de la *Préhistoire a La Kahina*, Editions Mimoun 1990

Derrick, Jonathan – *Africa's slaves today* – Schocken Books, New York. 1975.

Douglas Porch. - *The Conquest of the Sahara*. London Cape, 1985.

Ephraim Isaac - "Genesis, Judaism and the sons of Ham", pp 75-91 in John Ralph Willis, ed., *"Slaves and Slavery in Muslim Africa, Volume I: Islam and the Ideology of enslavement."* London Frank Cass, 1985.

Fevre, Francis. – "Les Seigneurs du Désert," *Histoire du Sahara*. Paris, 1983

Finley, M. L – *Ancient Slavery and Modern Ideology*. Viking Press, 1980.

Fisher and Fisher, Alan G. B. and Humphrey J. - "Slavery and Muslim Society in Africa. The Institution in Saharan and Sudanic Africa and the Trans-Saharan Trade. New York, Doubleday and company, 1971.

Gautier, E.F. – *History of North Africa from Arab conquest to 1830*. London, 1970.

Hakam, Yusuf – *Slavery in the Ottoman Empire and its Demise* (1800—1909) McMillian's Press, 1966.

Hawad, et Helene Claudot-Hawad - *Touaregs. Voix solitaires sous l'horizon confisqué*. 1996.

Herodotus – *The Histories*. Book IV, circa 430 BC.

Hope, Franklin J. – *From Slavery to Freedom*. New York Random House, 1969.

Hugot, Henri J. – *Le Sahara avant le Desert*. 1974.

Hugot, Henri, J. – *Dix Mille ans d'art et d'histoire du Sahara*

Hunwick, John – "Islamic Law and Polemics over Race and Slavery in North and West Africa (16-19th century), in *"Slavery in the Islamic Middle East,"* Shawn E. Marmon, Eds.

Jacques-Meunie, Mme. Dj. *"Hierarchie sociale au Maroc présaharien." Hesperis XLV 1958 pp 239-169.*

Lessard, Jean Michel – Sijilmassa, la ville et ses relations commerciales au XIe siècle d'après El Bekri, 1969.

Levtzion, Nehemia – The Jews of Sijilmassa and the Saharan Trade, in Abitbol, Communautés Juives, in *"Mélanges en hommage a Raymond Mauny," vol. 1.* 1981.

Lewis, Bernard – *Race and Slavery in the Middle East, a Historical* Enquiry – Oxford Press, 1990.

Lewis, Bernard – *Race and Color in Islam*, Harper and Row, 1971.

Lewis, Bernard – *Jews of Islam*, Princeton, 1984.

Lombard, M. – *The Golden Age of Islam*, 1975.

Lovejoy, Paul E - *Transformations in Slavery*, Cambridge, 1983.

Madden, John - *Slavery in the Roman Empire*, Numbers and Origins, 1996, Classics Ireland, Volume 3.

Marcais, G. – *Les Arabes en Berbérie du XIe au XIVe siècle*, 1913.

Marmon, Shawn E. (Ed) – *Slavery in the Islamic Middle East.*

Meillassoux, Claude – *L'esclavage en Afrique précoloniale*, Maspero, Paris 1975.

Meillassoux, Claude – *The anthropology of slavery*, Chicago, 1986.

Michaux-Bellaire, Demond – *L'esclavage au Maroc*, RMM XI, 1910. Pp 422-427.

Michel, Jonathan - "The Invasion of Songhay in 1591 and the Saadian Dynasty. An Examination of The Role of Europe in the Morocco Invasion of 1591 and the Rise to Power of the Saadian dynasty," 1995.

Murray, Gordon – *Slavery in the Muslim World*, 1987.

Norris, H. T. - *The Arab conquest of the Western Sahara*. Harlow, Essex. Longman, 1986.

Norris, H. T. – *The Berbers in Arabic Literature*, 1982.

Norris, H.T. – *The Tuaregs, their Islamic legacy and its diffusion in the Sahel*, 1975.

Oliel, Jacob – *Les Juifs au Sahara*

Porch, Douglas – *The conquest of the Sahara*, 1985.

Pottier, Ren – *Histoire du Sahara*

Renault, Francois – *La traite des Noirs au Proche-Orient Médiéval* VIIe-XIVe, Paris 1989.

Sengha, L. S. - *Négritude et Arabité*. Université du Caire, 1967.

Shawn E. Marmon, Editeur – Slavery In the Islamic Middle East. Markus Wiener Publishers, 1998.

Snowden, Frank M. – *Blacks in antiquity*. Harvard U. Press, 1970.

Starr, Chester – *The Ancient Greeks*. Oxford University Press, 1971

Stewart, C. C. – *Islam and social* order in Mauritania. Oxford, 1973.

Swanson, J. T – *The not yet Golden Trade*.

Tibry, Jacques – *Le Sahara Libyen dans l'Afrique du Nord Médiévale*, 1995.

Toledano, Ernest R. – *The Ottoman Slave Trade (1040-1890,)* 1962.

Vlahos, Olivia – *African Beginnings*, 1967.

Willis, John Ralph, Ed. - *Slaves and slavery in Muslim Africa*, Vol I – Frank Cass, 1985. a) "Jihad and the ideology of enslavement," and b) Ephraim Isaac:" Genesis, Judaism and the sons of Ham." In same volume, Willis, J. R. Ed.

Articles – Magazines, Journals, Internet:

Brett, Michael – "Islam and trade in Bilad-al Sudan," Journal of African History, 24 431-440, 1983.

Brett, Michael – "Ifriqya as a market for trans-Saharan Trade," Journal of African History, 10 347-364, 1969.

Brown, Kirsten – Slavery in Ancient Greece -

Chronology on Slavery by Richard E. Irby, Jr. (Feb. 23, 1994)

Ekeh, Peter – Course syllabus outline, "Africa and the Slave Trade," Department of African Studies, State University of New York at Buffalo, spring 1999.

La Traite des Noirs en 30 questions. "Pourquoi des captifs en Afrique? Bibliothèque du Ministère des Affaires Etrangères, Paris.

Le Monde Diplomatique – Avril 1998 pp 16-17 – "La Dimension Africaine de la Traite des Noirs." Elikia M'Bokolo

Madany, Shirley – Arabs and Slave Trade in "Answering Islam" Home Page.

Madden, John – Slavery in the Roman Empire, Numbers and Origins. University College, Galway, Ireland, 1996.

Manning, Patrick – "Slavery in Africa," Essay on Africana.com

Masomem, Pekka – "Trans-Saharan Trade and the West African Discovery of the Mediterranean World, "Third Nordic Conference on Middle Eastern Studies, Finland 1995.

Mazrui, Ali – Voice of America – Interview - Islam in Africa, Part II, 1997.

McDougall, E. A. – "The view from Awdaqhust, war, trade, and social change in the southwestern Sahara from the 8th to 15th century, "Journal of African History, 26 1-22, 1985.

Michel, Jonathan – *The Moroccan invasion of Sudan in 1591 and the Saadian dynasty.* (1995)

Mississippi State University Conference – Identifying Enslaved Africans, 1997. (The Slave Route in the Islamic World -)

Myers, John B. – History 3115, Columbus State University Reading List: Part I – African Slave Trade.

Paul, Charles B. Article in The Textbook Letter (1995): "Where did Slavery come from?"

Progler, Yusuf - Muslim Media – Islam and the politics of slavery in American Academia, June 1999.

UNESCO DOCUMENTS:

Akomolafe, Femi – On Slavery, 1994. **UNESCO** Saharan Slave Route project.

Devisse, J. – "Trade and Trade routes in West Africa," **UNESCO**. General history of Africa, Volume III, ch. 14, 1988.

Mouralis, Bernard: "L'Esclavage vu de l'Afrique", May 1998 – **UNESCO**

Saharan Trade: A Link Between Europe and Africa –**UNESCO**.

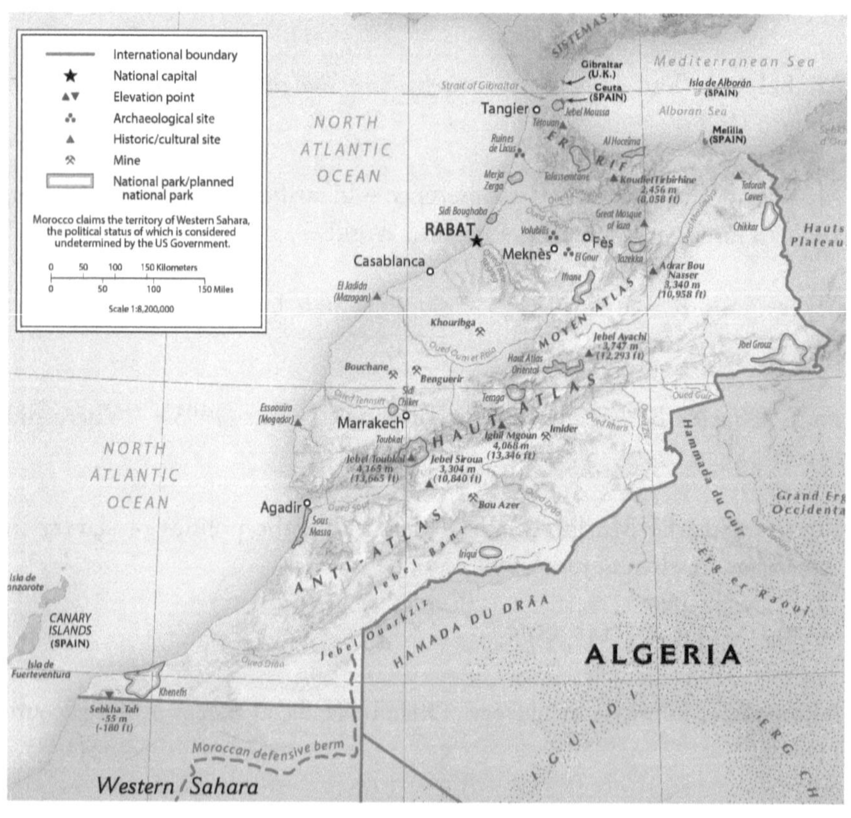

Map of Morocco

The growth of the argan tree is strictly limited to the southwest region of Morocco, from the Atlantic Ocean to the Draa Valley, in the Souss Valley and the Atlas Mountain foothills., south of Essaouira and north of Tiznit.

The Argan Tradition Of Southwestern Morocco

The Argan tree (Argana Spinosa) is indigenous to the Valley of the Souss and to the lower slopes of the Atlas Mountains of southwest Morocco. This remarkable tree of the Sapotacea family is unique to the region and grows nowhere else in the world. Argan groves cover approximately 43% of the land area in that region of Morocco. From time immemorial, the argan woodlands have functioned both as a literal anchor against the winds and erosion of the soil, and a cultural one around which a pastoral way of life and a traditional home industry of oil extraction from its nuts have characterized the Amazigh community of this territory.

The ecological, social and cultural values of the argan tree constitute one of North Africa's unique and most precious natural resources. It has insured the subsistence of some two million Imazighen in this predominantly rural area of Morocco.

Targant (feminine appellation in Tachelhit)

"Old Argan Tree, you are the most resistant and without doubt the most beautiful of all trees."

The Argan tree, or Moroccan ironwood, is an evergreen spiny tree, which grows in groves throughout the landscape of southwest Morocco from Safi southward as Goulimine, and eastward through the Souss Valley and Tafraoute where the strongest specimens are found. The tree dates from the geological Tertiary Era, grows slowly and survives sometimes for centuries. The median lifetime of trees is 150 to 200 years, with the oldest ranging from 200 to 400 years. The tree does not grow below the altitude of 500-600 meters, and above that of 2,000 meters (approximately 1650 to 6500 feet) with most of its growth concentrated in the foothills of the Atlas Mountains. The argan forest covers an area of about 320,000 square miles and numbers some 20 million trees.

The trunk of the tree is gnarly. Its sturdy and deep roots retain the soil against constant erosion, allowing penetration and retention of moisture in a land that receives little rainfall. It allows other species to grow in its shade. Its wood is used in construction. Its nuts are harvested in a unique manner through the agency of tree-climbing goats. The argan oil extracted from the processed nuts is of an exquisite quality and taste, and it is used locally both for its nutritional properties and its medicinal virtues. Argan by-products which are left at the bottom of the press during the process of oil extraction ("targemmut") are also essential as fuel and fodder for the animals.

The tree is key to the ecological stability of the region. Today, the ancient knowledge of its nutritional and medicinal properties has grown beyond the local community, and reached the international scene. It is sought after for cosmetic purposes in numerous beauty and bath products, as well as for culinary ends. While many plants have significant impact for the health of indigenous peoples throughout the world, few of them acquire any reputation outside the local native populations of an eco-system in which they thrive, where a traditional use of native species is maintained. Argan oil has achieved international notoriety.

Today, the argan tree is acquiring somewhat of a reputation outside Morocco. The recent story of the development and increase of the traditional oil extraction industry is a remarkable one. It owes a great deal to one woman, Dr. Zoubida Charrouf, of the Chemistry Department of the Mohamed V University, in Rabat. This story, and that of the Amazigh women involved in it, is a superb example of cultural and economic development based on traditional knowledge and practice in the modern world.

The Collect of the Argan Fruit ("Tigri") and Traditional Oil Extraction

The fruit of the argan tree is the size of an apricot or a plum, and its white pulp envelops a hard-shelled kernel which contains from one to three pits, or almonds. The fruit matures between May and July. A tree's average yield is about eight kilos per year.

Traditionally, herds of climbing goats are taken to argan groves in the spring, and allowed to gorge themselves on the fruit; then, they are led home in the evening where they are plied with lots of water, making them regurgitate the almonds. These nuts are believed to be far superior to those which would have been harvested by human hands. The form of collective gathering of the fruit by hand, ("ar garrun ifeyyachen," local term in the region of Essaouira among the Haha Ayt Yasin) is authorized by local assemblies after the fruit is allowed to ripen, and occurs in July. Public criers relay the decision taken by the notables of the assemblies, shouting from village to village: "The Argan is authorized." The fruit is collected with special offerings called "isisel" to dispel all bad influences, carried in baskets and taken home to process, ultimately furnishing the oil.

First the fruit is dried. Then, the pits are extracted and cracked open ("arrag") on a special flat stone ("asarg n warrag"). The action of breaking the nut ("aqqa") is called "irga." The flat, hard stone upon which the nuts are cracked is called "assarwag." The argan nut which has been shelled of its almond, "tizenin," that is the pitted fruit, is called "irgn." Today, the dried fruit can also be bought in local markets and shelled by women who specialize in the task.

The subsequent part of the process of oil extraction comes with the toasting of the skinned almonds by the Amazigh women. The roasted nuts are pounded and mixed with a little warm water and kneaded into a brownish dough ("ar zemman tazgmmut") which is pressed through a traditional millstone, following certain ritual procedures, with incantations and offerings to insure its beneficial properties.

An offering of a few drops in the four directions is essential before the consumption of the new oil. The obtained oil is one of the purest oils in the world, with remarkable properties. The by-products of this extraction are used for the making of "amlou" (a rich mixture of ground nuts, oil and honey generally consumed at breakfast), and fodder for the animals. The leftover substance which is fed to the cattle is called "tawrrit."

Until recently, the lengthy and time-consuming process of argan oil extraction was home based and labor intensive. It is estimated, for instance, that the collection of argan fuel wood amounts to 800,000 working days a year, while the extraction of oil itself is approximately 20,000,000 working days. One hundred kilograms of nuts are needed to produce one to two kilograms of oil. Another set of statistics indicates that it takes at least two working days to produce one liter of argan oil. Traditional use of the argan oil is domestic, nutritional, medicinal, and cosmetic. Locally, it is used as a skin emollient and against arthritis, and secondarily as massage oil and beauty aid. Another use of the oil is for home soap making, and the tree has been found indeed to be rich in saponins in recent chemical analysis. Saponins are natural detergents found in certain plant, mainly in desert plants, with cholesterol-lowering properties. With the advent of oil producing co-ops in the region of Essaouira, it is estimated that the yearly production of oil for that region is about 1,000 to 2,000 tons.

Symbolic value of the Argan

The argan tree has marked the lives and imagination of the Amazigh people of this territory for centuries. It has inspired poetry, art forms, and local stories. It is a symbol of local culture, inextricably linked to Amazigh cultural identity in the Souss Valley and around Agadir and Essaouira. It represents the natural health of the land, the people, and their cultural survival. Even if the tourists who flock today to the super resorts of the coastal areas do not know of this wealth, the ancient world was not totally ignorant of the value of argan oil. Written records of its extraction date back to the thirteenth century, and the oil was exported to Europe in the eighteenth century. It was supplanted by the popularity of the olive oil, less nutty in its flavor. The argan oil has a distinctive flavor, somewhat akin to that of walnut oil. There are degrees of purity, and the purest is highly valued. It is not recommended to purchase argan oil on the open market or the side of the rod, as such oil is impure, having been mixed with other oils, and it is often degraded by the lack of hygiene with which it is bottled in recycled containers. The shelf life of argan oil is relatively short.

The Argan oil enters the global market

The active ingredients of argan oil were not identified until modern chemistry took a look; the work of a dedicated Moroccan chemist, Dr. Zoubida Charrouf has deeply influenced the argan oil industry of the region. She has been called "The Champion of the Argan Tree." It is her curiosity which led her to identify the anti-oxidant properties of the oil. She was instrumental in the creation of co-ops of women to process the extraction of the oil in large quantities. The oil produced by these co-ops, entirely under the direction of women, is bottled according to international standards as to purity and health. The co-op of Tidzi was founded in 1998, and that of Tamanar in 2000. In 2001, the AMAL co-op of Tamanar received an international Biodiversity Award. By all standards, this business is successful, employing some fifty women full-time in the factories, and over 120 women working part-time in their homes. Today, they are also engaged in the production of cosmetics based on the oil.

Though the argan tree constitutes a national treasure, more than one third of the argan woodlands has disappeared in the last one hundred years. It is estimated that where a hundred trees once stood, only thirty now survive. In the last ten years, several projects have been undertaken to preserve their unique eco-system, and the Amazigh cultural heritage associated with this ancient forest.

The Importance of International Alliances for the Amazigh Movement of North Africa

Presented at the United Nations, 2002 P.I.P.E. Conference in preparation of the First Session of The Permanent Forum on Indigenous Issues. Unlike other Essays in this book, this text was an oral presentation, and the following remarks therefore represent notes rather than a more formal Essay. A few additional comments have been added post-facto.

In this presentation, I will first introduce the Imazighen and the Amazigh culture of the thirty million or so autochthonous people of North Africa. I will review the various local, national and international branches of our fast growing international movement, and the manner in which means of communication and international alliances have formed and serve the communities of base in North Africa and sub-Saharan countries, the "Diaspora" of Europe, and the Amazigh communities of Canada and the United States.

In addition, the presentation will summarize the various technologies (use of the internet, digital technology and emerging forms of expression) with which the Tazzla Institute has worked in the past ten years in order to publicize various aspects of the Amazigh culture and inscribe this culture in the record of history, in the United States and abroad.

THE TAZZLA INSTITUTE: Functions and Role

The Tazzla Institute was initially created to support American Indian groups and issues, environmental issues, and subsequently Amazigh issues by its activities. In 1997, the Institute began a series of television programs, called **"Tamazgha, Berber Land of Morocco,"** following a trip to the south and the pre-Sahara region of Morocco. Ten half-hour television programs are available, which are the only Amazigh television programs available in the United States. They have been followed by other programs on Amazigh gatherings in the US, and recently to bring to the attention of American viewers the struggle of our people throughout North Africa. **(Amazigh News, 2001-2007)**

In 1998, the Institute became aware of an Amazigh Internet Forum, the Amazigh-net, which opened up fields of communication, participation, research, and advocacy impossible before. We came immediately in touch with the World Amazigh Congress (CMA) which was preparing its first International World gathering in Tafira, Canary Islands. Members of the Institute traveled there not only to become part of this international movement and meet a number of its representatives, but also to videotape the whole event for the CMA. A short, edited version of this momentous event is made available through the television program entitled "Amazigh Identity."

Since those first steps, which aimed at educating the American public about Amazigh issues and human rights and a little known culture, the Institute has progressed on the national and international levels, through the agencies of links with other Amazigh organizations, Internet sites journals and magazines. The TAZZLA INSTITUTE became a member of the Amazigh International coalition for the Defense of Human Rights, and has sponsored the NGO organization OVD Tidhelt of Niger in the United States, as "Engaged Partner" to that Tuareg grass-root organization since 1999.

THE AMAZIGH NETWORK: Local, national, and international

1. The social structures of the Amazigh Movement.

The Amazigh society distinguishes itself by democratic rule and the traditional social structure of the Assembly of Elders, where counsel is taken for common action in all matters, at the level of the village, then the valley, and thirdly the region. When matters become of great importance to the people, this Assembly of elders becomes a general alliance of the Councils where deputies from the village have elected a representative to the valley and to the regional level become national Council members. Thus, on a national level, spokespersons representing the group, the valley and the villages of the valley are empowered to make decisions.

In today's world, these councils have taken the form of "cultural associations" which sprang in the underground of a nation where oppressive policies forbade free speech and right of assemblies for Imazighen. They became the focal points of cultural survival and a struggle, which has gone from the base of the people in rural areas, to the valley or locality level, then to national headquarters. A good example of such structure and function is the TAMAYNUT Association in Morocco, with over thirty branches at the local level, and a headquarter in Rabat, the royal capital of the kingdom of Morocco. Similar cultural associations, but with less spreading influence are AMREC (Moroccan Amazigh Center for Research and Education) and the Association of the University of Agadir, with membership from various regions of Morocco.

Similar cultural associations have sprung throughout Europe in various countries. With over a million and a half "Berbers' (primarily Kabyles of Algeria) in France, cultural associations in France abound. But there are very active organizations in London, the Netherlands, Belgium, Italy, Germany and Spain. There is a vibrant Kabyle community of Imazighen in Canada and in the United States, A.C.A.A., The Amazigh Cultural Association in America, is the oldest association.

2. The international alliances of the Amazigh Movement.

Representatives of TAMAYNUT have acted on the international level, and are active in an International Amazigh Coalition, which includes a number of associations from various countries of Africa, such as Tunisia, Algeria, Morocco, the Canary Islands, Mali, and Burkina-Faso. Representatives of TAMAYNUT are equally active with the World Amazigh Congress, (C.M.A.) another international NGO organization of the Amazigh Movement, headquartered in France, which has met with Mary Robinson, Human Rights Commissioner, and representatives of the European Parliament, with the support of The Green Party of Europe. Both Tamaynut and C.M.A. participated in the recent global conference Against Racism and Discrimination, which took place in South Africa last August 2001.

3. **Means of Communication in networking and alliance formation:**

The Amazigh Movement has the peculiar characteristic of numbering a large number of communications engineers in its midst. In the United States, there are indeed many communication specialists, and Amazigh students in American universities who will enter the ranks of electronic communication specialists outnumber all other fields.

The primary impetus came from the set-up of the Amazigh-net, a Forum devised by a member of ACAA, an engineer in communication presently living in San Diego, California, and the tremendous growth of this internet exchange used for news dissemination, cultural exchanges, and the call to various alerts, petitions, etc. The Amazigh-net has been at the forefront of an explosion of means of communication for the Amazigh Movement.

In the last ten years, numerous sites began to open, such as Kabyle.com, Berberworld.com, and in the United States W.A.A.C in Washington, the World Amazigh Action Coalition, which has played an important function in education, information dissemination, and activism. Libyans got into action more recently and created Libyamazigh.net. The Assembly of Elders of Kabylia, Algeria, opened its own site to inform Imazighen around the world of their moves and decisions concerning the grave situation in Algeria.

After the assassination of Lounes Matoub, the great singer/advocate of the Algerian Amazigh movement, the Lounes Foundation opened a web site. More recently, a community of the Aures Mountains of Algeria announced the opening of a very interesting new site. The TEMUST Tuareg site set up by Abdahali Attayoub of Lyon, France has already a certain longevity and promotes Tuareg culture and Human Rights Publications in Berber language, Tamazight, began to open their doors, as press restrictions began to weaken in Morocco. Still, as the Moroccan government does not financially support either press, radio and television other than Arabic ones, the funds necessary to the healthy operation of these instruments of communication are minimal, private, and often, lacking. Finally, one of the latest born, but not the least, as it allowed rural people of Algeria and Morocco to equip themselves with satellites and tune-in to their favorite Amazigh television programs, is BRTV, the French Amazigh Television and Radio Channel which is the jewel created by a French Berber Jurist, the same problem of financial viability affects BRTV which relies on membership donations for operation.

A list of numerous other sites can be obtained by using a search engine for "Berber" or "Amazigh" sites.

The Amazigh Movement and other Indigenous peoples

We have already noted that The Amazigh Movement has networked with numerous other indigenous organizations through its NGO groups at the United Nations, with other autochthonous people through the Working Group on Indigenous People, and personal friendships with American Indian representatives of the United States and Canada.

In the USA, Tazzla Institute has worked at the United Nations for several years, participating in a joint NGO project under the UNESCO Culture for Peace Program, "Creating Peace Through the Arts." Under this project, Tazzla Institute has introduced a number of speakers at various occasions in the past five years. In 2006, it brought Dounia BenJelloun, the director of the newly created Dounia Productions of Casablanca, Morocco to introduce a remarkable documentary filmed by a famous French film director, Jacques Renoir, titled "The Amazigh Renaissance" on the teaching of Tamazight by means of the ancestral script of Tifinagh in rural schools of Morocco.

The Tazzla Institute also has a history of working with American Indian groups, among which the International Indian Treaty Council, an NGO which recently obtained an Eco/Soc status at the United Nations. The Tazzla Institute has fostered ties between this organization and the Amazigh Movement. Recently, for the first time, a United Nations Liaison

Officer for IITC requested through the agency of the Tazzla Institute documentation from the Amazigh Movement for an intervention including Imazighen.

Uses of technology in gathering and diffusing information locally, and globally.

Tazzla Institute for Cultural Diversity instituted the project Amazigh Video Productions to create documentaries on the Amazigh culture and Imazighen which have been aired in California, several events in the US. as well as in Morocco.

The 11 programs which began to air in San Francisco in 1998 as Tamazgha, Berber Land of Morocco, were also shown on community Television channels in Los Angeles, and are presently available in digital format to use in classrooms and for other cultural presentations. In addition, Amazigh Video Productions created another series of programs from its Los Angeles headquarters (2001-2007) reporting on important Human Rights issues relevant to Algerian, Moroccan and Saharan groups under the title of "Amazigh News" The list of those half-hour reports is available on our web site at http://www.tazzla.org, video section.

International contacts realized through the medium of the internet and linking with other web sites has brought Helene Hagan and Tazzla Institute in touch with a number of individuals and groups willing to help the Amazigh cause. In 2005-2006, a book was created to help the Desert Schools of the Sahara in Niger, entitled "Tuareg Jewelry, Traditional Symbols and Patterns" (XLibris, 2006.)

This book made the most of electronic technology by gathering information and digital photography on the internet, with the collaboration of a number of helpful individuals and organizations interested in helping the Amazigh cause. The book is published on demand through the latest cutting edge technology provided by the publishing industry, by Xlibris, a branch of Random House Publishers.

Conclusion

The structures of the Amazigh Movement and the networks in which it inserts itself are both regional - Africa, Europe, Northern America and trans-regional. The foundation of the Movement is the Amazigh individual, enamored of freedom and always ready to struggle for democratic institutions. The people come together at the village level, and look to alliances, which have been in the long traditional past of our culture viable instruments of self-rule. These structures are used to delegate representatives to larger social contexts, and finally, in the age of global communication, to interact not only with other groups of Imazighen, but with indigenous people of Africa and the world at large.

The ability to network outside countries of North Africa which until recently were under the rule of Arabic powers intent upon suppressing Amazigh expression without possibility to inform and be informed by outside opinion, has helped the Amazigh Movement in untold ways. In turn, the freedom of expression obtained outside the traditional territory and the growing use of a global internet use and network have had incalculable impact upon the people at home, their determination to obtain the most basic rights, and the conduct of official regimes toward these populations.

BOOK REVIEW ONE

The Berbers (The People of Africa) Michael Brett and Elizabeth Fentress

-Blackwell Publishers (1998)

Presented as a work of collaboration between an archaeologist and a historian, (Fentress and Brett respectively), this book is an overview of the history of the Amazigh people of North Africa, known as Berbers. The authors precede their review of this history with the comment that no such "general book on the Berbers is available in English," and a peculiar observation on page seven of their introduction that "the role of Berbers as protagonists in their own history has been lost in the process." This remark prompted the incorporation of biographical details of my own story as a Berber scholar, which are essentially addressed to the question of a Berber voice in history and anthropology. The general review of materials relative to Berber culture is, in my opinion, the overwhelming value of the book's contribution. The presentation is an overview of the existing literature on a group of people ignored by most British and American anthropologists and historians. Most of their references in the extensive bibliography are French.

As a Berber of Kabyle (Algerian) ancestry, born and raised in the interior of Morocco around the time of World War II, I found myself soundly dissuaded from pursuing a Berber Project at Stanford University when studying for my doctorate degree. It seemed that no one on my Ph.D. Committee, (or in the whole Anthropology department of this major American university), knew anything about Berber people. My 1981 Spring Paper, which was supposed to precede my dissertation, was entitled Tazz'unt: Ritual, Ecology, and Social Order in a Valley of the High Atlas of Morocco. In my paper I explained that the Berbers were a sizeable indigenous population of North Africa, that they exist in segmentary tribal structures and that they observe a politically important maraboutic cult. I explained that the Berbers are an important group as they act as a powerful factor in preventing tyrannical rule and maintaining order in the tribal context. My spring paper additionally addressed the Spring Berber ritual of the region (Tazz'unt)* as one specific instance of a rich context of living Berber traditions. This element, interestingly, was not found in the book, The Berbers by Brett and Fentress.

My own 1982 research paper was skeptically reviewed and dismissed by commentators who admitted their ignorance of some of the same issues presented in it. By their own admission, the reviewers of my Spring Paper declared they could not weigh the value of such works as the History of Ibn Khaldun, the theory of checks and balances advanced by Robert Montagne, or other numerous French and North African reputable sources which I amply presented (all used, incidentally, by Brett and Fentress). There was even a suggestion, to my intense dismay, that I could have invented some of the symbolic aspects of this tradition as my reviewers could not check the inside view of the ritual, which involved Berber informants of the High Atlas village (Hassan Jouad and others). I was advised to contribute to American Anthropology through another area of research and specialization.

In Morocco, during preliminary fieldwork, I encountered deep antagonism on the part of the representative of the Moroccan Minister of Culture to whom I introduced myself in 1981. The message he conveyed to me in clear language was that there were no longer any Berbers in Morocco and that I had been misinformed. Of course, the Arabic gentleman knew nothing of my birthplace or ethnic origin, or of my personal ties to the Berber community. Upon my remark that I would rent a car and travel through the High Atlas of Morocco to see for myself, he replied that I would be kept under surveillance, and if I tried to do that, I would have the option between imprisonment and deportation. These unveiled threats were made in the privacy of our interview in his office of Assistant Minister of Culture in Rabat, and I can still vividly recall the glacial stare of that Arab across his desk. I spent the summer of 1981 in Casablanca in the relative safety of my brother's home (it was a time of riots in five Moroccan cities), learning from friends, chance encounters and the majority of taxi drivers (all Berbers) that Imazighen (Berbers) were indeed very much alive but denied official existence by stringent politics of Arabization. Upon my return to Stanford, I switched specialization and worked thereafter with Oglala Lakota people of the Pine Ridge Indian Reservation in South Dakota. While never forgetting my life-long determination of keeping alive the flame of my Berber culture, I submitted a paper on the Oral Tradition of the Lakota for a Master's Degree, knowing that a doctorate dissertation focused on my Berber culture was doomed, despite the fact that all other academic requirements for a Ph.D. degree had been met.

After devoting a number of years to the work of human rights, ecological and social issues of American Indians in South Dakota and California (I served as Historic Preservation Officer for the Federated Coast Miwok of Marin and Sonoma Counties for a few years), the computer and the internet broadened my horizon and furnished me with the exhilarating experience of linking with a network of Berber activists and the International Berber Movement. The Movement was founded in Europe by a majority of Algerian Kabyles, at the very moment I was walking through the beloved mountains of my native land again. This time, I proceeded on my own and went with video camera in hand to record landscapes, music, and people of the High Atlas and the pre-Sahara regions of Morocco-without the academic obligation to notify the Moroccan authorities of my whereabouts or my work.

I am now an active member of the Amazigh Cultural Association in America, joining my brothers and sisters, Kabyles, Shawya, Chleuhs, Riffi, Tuaregs, Canarians, Siwans, and others grouped in cultural associations springing throughout Tamazgha from Egypt to the Canary Islands of the Atlantic Ocean. This Berber territory of North Africa, "Tamazgha," is the topic of the book under review.

———

Let me say that, as a Berber woman and an anthropologist, I have mixed feelings about this book. Indeed, I find it valuable for an introductory class on Amazigh culture. I would not hesitate to make it a basic requirement for such a course in the U.S. However, I would have to correct some information, and add a great deal. Certain key elements are completely missing. There are, to name but a few:

a. The pre-historical or proto-historical period presented by the authors lacks depth and ignores some of the latest findings. On page 25, for instance, the authors write that as early as the end of the fourth century we begin to hear of Libyan "kings" such as Aelymas. As such kingdoms emerged throughout the Mediterranean in the Hellenistic age, the Berbers followed suit, the authors advance... Recent research and published findings have demonstrated the presence of great Libyan Kings and dynasties preceding the advent of the Egyptian Pharaonic era, which has been set at about 3,000 B.C. The discovery of the Libyan Stone, presently called The Palermo Stone (from the name of the museum where it is preserved), helped change the horizon of researchers: this stone lists a lineage of fifty Libyan Kings antecedent to the Pharaonic line. These Libyan Kingdoms extended to the Nile, the Fayum area west of the Nile and the Western region of the Delta. The presence of Libyco-Berber populations from the Sahara desert to the Maghreb in the West and to the Delta and the Fayum Lake in the East are documented as far as 4,500 B.C., with pottery, agriculture, and domestication of cattle present from the regions of the Fezzan to the banks of the Nile. Indeed, there are indications that the first King who unified Egypt was a descendant from this Libyan (Libyco-Berber) lineage.

b. Pages 27 to 31 attempt to address the matter of burial complexes and funerary practices, but the information is substantially thin and at times misleading. An excellent study of Berber funerary monuments in the south of Morocco and pre-Sahara, and their physical and semantic relationship to funerary practices of the pyramidal age of Egypt was published by Mohammed Chafik of the Royal Academy of Morocco in 1997. Brett and Fentress do mention the extent of archaeological data such as the 60,000 tombs located in the Fezzan area of the Sahara desert, but do not expand on their data. They instead concentrate on funerary monuments of a much later period, which indicate Hellenistic influence, and conclude that this type of monument was modeled after the "Greek Heroon" or hero's monument. No evidence is put forward to present the rich data of funerary practices of the Berbers from the Sahara to the banks of the Nile prior to that era, except in isolated statements which are not followed by pertinent information of a precise nature. On page 33, we find a rare isolated remark on the practice of incubation related to the cult of ancestors (pre Greco-Roman): As Camps has shown, provision of chambers for this practice is a standard trait of Berber tombs, from prehistory onwards. And, a little further, inexplicably since pertinent data has been omitted, the concluding remark: "It is not surprising that tombs are the major monuments left by the Berber Kings. Although their form is Hellenistic, their massive size suggests that the dead kings occupied a role as super ancestors." Such a statement ignores the entire body of data preceding the arrival of the Greeks and Romans in North Africa which is attached to the very African cult of ancestors. It again stresses the Hellenistic aspect of the architecture of a tomb or two instead of the probable continuity of archaic general practice through the times of colonization of Africa. Berber funerary practices seem to have extended from the Atlantic Ocean to the banks of the Nile consistently, and might have given rise to the later "Egyptian" funerary rites and the whole pyramidal complex (Cf. Mohammed Chafik, Revue Tifinagh, No. 11-12, 1997, pages 89-98: Elements lexicaux Berbères pouvant apporter un éclairage dans la recherche des origines préhistoriques des pyramides). Such research, stemming from North African scholars, seems to be unavailable to the authors of the book.

c.   The Jewish Berber population has been grossly ignored. I am not referring to the late exodus of Jews from Spain during the time of Inquisition, which was not essentially Berber, even though it must be stressed that a substantial component of the Iberian Peninsula population had indeed been "berberized" from the time of Berber military occupation from the eighth century onward. There was conversion of entire Berber tribes to Judaism before Christianity or Islam reached North Africa. There is ample evidence of very ancient Judaic societies in villages of the Anti Atlas and the pre

Sahara region in particular, but also in the Middle Atlas region of Morocco. I am not so familiar with the Algerian and Tunisian components of Tamazgha, but similar pockets of Jewish Berber people existed in those regions.

d. There is no mention at all by Brett and Fentress of The Canary Islands as originally peopled by Berbers, and of the archaeology, music, whistled language, and customs still in evidence today in those islands, situating the several Canary Islands, with topographical names still entirely Berber, squarely in the Berber territory of Tamazgha. In the linguistic map showing this territory, the Canary Islands are not included by Brett and Fentress, which is not entirely correct, for if the language is no longer spoken there, the topography definitely reflects Berber terminology. Also, there is a strong Canary Island component to the present-day Berber cultural movement, and efforts at revitalizing the Tamazight language is lost on the islands, following the model of the revitalization of Hebrew in Israel. The omission of the Canary Islands in the history of Berbers is a glaring one.

e. There is no mention in the book of the important figure of Ma El Ainin, a charismatic Holy Man, Prophet and Warrior who galvanized the south of Morocco against foreign invasion in the early part of the twentieth century. His tomb in Tiznit (Anti-Atlas region of Morocco) is revered and attended strictly by women. He has direct descendants alive today with great "baraka" (power of sanctity.) The omission of Ma El Ainin and his founding of Samara, the city of brotherhood constructed and managed according to the values of the desert that was ransacked in the first entry of Europeans in the south of Morocco, is a notable one, in my opinion. Ma El Ainin had a profound historical impact in the entire region. It could be that the collective memory of Ma-El-Ainin is mostly an oral one, ignored in the European literature which seems to be the primary source of information for Brett and Fentress.

The history presented by Brett and Fentress is not only omitting some crucial elements to Berber culture, but it also suffers from its bookish origins, leaving this reader with a feeling of being subjected at times to opinions gathered somewhere else and presented as facts. This can be serious. For instance, I lived in Morocco during the years of turmoil during

Independence. We knew, family and friends, that Morocco was never "pacified" by General Lyautey as the French official story would advance. Inland Berbers (Imazighen) never submitted. The depiction of the role of Thami El Glaoui, the Pasha of Marrakesh, in this process, seems far too thin, and his hasty dismissal from the historical scene plainly arrogant. The Berber leader was a very controversial figure of the era, and yielded great power indeed. He was directly instrumental to the return of Sultan Mohammed V from his exile in Madagascar, where he had been banished by French politicians with The Glaoui's assent. The text reads, page 191:

Thami El Glaoui ... "was exposed as a man of straw, his empire in the south a hollow mockery of his power in the past..." a quotation said to arise from the reading of Maroc authored by Julien. Such an extrapolation and cavalier evaluation is, in the face of ample documentation on the Glaoui family, a distortion of history. Berber historians will no doubt review the complex role and personality of this towering figure of the twentieth century. He was no man of straw, by any standard, before, after, or during his planned and public submission to the throne. His powerful alliances and astute politics need to be weighed far more subtlety in the context of the French colonization period. This formidable Berber warrior, politician, and leader, who steered the politics of Morocco for over half a century, consciously made a decision for the benefit of all Moroccans as a very old man on the brink of death. Morocco and its freedom from the yoke of Europe was his goal. He knew that by asking the French allies to return the Sultan from exile, this Sultan would follow age-old practices of eliminating him, the Glaoui, and his family from positions of power in Morocco, and that his vast holdings would be confiscated. Thami El Glaoui may have been a controversial figure, but he was not the fool the authors of this book present to the readers without any explanatory detail to demonstrate why he is called a "man of straw". Such a travesty of history is not permissible in a scholarly work. It is here that I must express perhaps my most severe comments. In this particular page of history which is well known to me, personally, as well as in scholarly terms. I read with grave concern the following text:

"Just as the Berbers had been invented by the Arabs for the purpose of the Arab conquest and the Arab empire, so now they were finally resurrected by the French as a subject race to be kept apart from their Arab neighbors in the interest of French hegemony. A hundred years after the process began in Algeria, it was brought to conclusion in Morocco with the creation of what Berque called a national park whose inhabitants were so many sequoias, a protected species on which the French hoped to rely in their dealings with the untrustworthy Arabs of the plains and the cities." (Note: J. Berque, French North Africa, London 1967, page 219.) For more than in Algeria, they turned ironically to the old Kabyles, those ancient enemies of direct rule, to buttress their government of the country as a whole". (Note: Cf. Bidwell, Morocco under Colonial Rule, pages 293-301.)

What we have in this paragraph is some opinion emitted by Brett mirroring other opinions emitted by Berque and Bidwell. The thought advanced in this language that the Berbers were invented by the Arabs for the purpose of their conquest is refuted by the documented presence of Berbers in North Africa for centuries before the arrival of the Arabs. Such a statement has been paralleled by the assertion that Christopher Columbus "discovered" America, as if American Indians had not been conscious of their existence and the territory they occupied before his arrival. In the case of Berbers, the assertion is even more ludicrous as there is ample history recorded of the flourishing tribes and kingdoms of North Africa, long before Arabs reached that part of the world, around 700 A.D. Secondly, the Berbers - Imazighen or Free Human Beings - did not wait for the French to be "resurrected", as the French troops learned in their military encounters with a country-wide resistance. The entire tribal territory of Morocco was called to unite under total alliance against the external threat represented by the French troops, a traditional and formal Berber War Alliance called "leff". The French had been called to intervene in the affairs of Morocco by the Sultan of Morocco at the turn of the twentieth century because the reigning Arabic monarch was unable to impose his will on the numerous Berber tribes of the interior mountains. French troops came in with heavy artillery and powerful guns, leaving a bloody trail which testified to the passion and fierce opposition of the Berber people. The French did not "resurrect" the Berbers but massacred them by tens of thousands, buying some, manipulating the politics of their leaders, often setting one leader against another (a well-known policy) nearly destroying Berber societies. Any Berber knows that trail of blood. To speak of resurrection is a blasphemy, even if - and certainly it is not specified in the text by Brett - it is meant to refer to the "Dahir Berbère", (French Decree which recognized the precedence of Tribal Law) and which granted tribal Berbers customary law as opposed to the Coranic Law which was observed in the Arabic coastal areas and cities of Morocco. It was a temporary political strategy rather than a granting of life on the part of the inept French generals and politicians who succeeded each other rapidly in that period called the Protectorate of Morocco. Moroccans, Arabs and Berbers, always knew for a fact that there was never a "pacification" of Morocco, even if that term sounded good in official speeches and in French reports.

Clear as it may be, it must be emphasized that in order to be resurrected, one must die first, and to characterize the Berber populations of Morocco or their traditions as dead before the arrival of the French is nonsensical, particularly in the light of affirming that the Dahir Berbère legitimized their de facto existing traditional Law. The French benefited from upholding these practices in their overall politics in the region. They entered into multiple diplomatic alliances with powerful Berber leaders of the Middle Atlas, of the Ait Atta formidable Confederacy, and others who had large holdings of land, immense resources, and extensive tribal groups throughout the southern lands, in order to maintain a militarily established control over the territory of Morocco. It is true that the Commander of the troops, General Lyautey, seemed to have been surprised and impressed by the extent of Berber traditions, but such factor would only go to reinforce the fact that Berber cultures were indeed there to surprise and impress him.

Finally, I do not even understand the last sentence of that paragraph: "For more than in Algeria, they turned ironically to the old Kabyles, those old enemies of direct rule, to buttress their government of the country as a whole." Who are the old Kabyles of Morocco the French turn to? Could the unfortunate use of the word "Kabyles" be mistaken and mean the various powers, Caids and Pashas of Berber confederacies just mentioned? Kabylia is in Algeria, and apart from very few Kabyle individuals like my grandfather who emigrated to a Moroccan city with his family in 1920, there are no Kabyle groups in any part of the land of Morocco the French could turn to in order to reinforce their rule. There is a definite misunderstanding or error of terms which slipped in at the conclusion of this strange paragraph.

While acknowledging again that this book is a worthy effort in a vacuum of information about Amazigh culture in the Anglo-Saxon world, I must reiterate that my mixed feelings of both elated recognition of the subject matter of this book, and uneasiness bordering at times toward estrangement from the perspective of its authors, persisted and even amplified at a second reading.

Mausoleum of Maréchal Lyautey, Gardens of La Résidence, Rabat, 1953 – The Mausoleum no longer exists The remains of the first Resident General of France in Morocco were removed and are now reposing in state at the Museum of the Invalides, in Paris. *(Family photo)*

BOOK REVIEW TWO

"Amazigh Arts in Morocco. Women shaping Berber Identity," by Cynthia Becker (2006)

The title promises more than the book delivers. First, it is not a book on Amazigh Arts in Morocco; it is a book primarily devoted to the description of weddings and marriage ritual among the Ayt Khabbash, a group of Ait Atta in the Tafilalet region of southeastern Morocco. Second, it is not a book about Berber identity, as Amazigh identity and its symbolism are not specifically linked to gender, but are shaped by a number of factors not examined in this book. The analysis lacks in historical depth, political and economic dimensions; it also ignores the role and influence of Islam and religious ideology in the shaping of the mores and traditions the author attempts to present. All such factors are indeed of crucial importance to the understanding of human relations in a region known for its extremely stratified society. From this book, the reader cannot form a clear picture of such a society. Despite such lacks, the book offers excellent data, and is obviously the result of close relationships over a certain period of time between the author and a number of Ayt Khabbash women. It also offers a welcome feminine perspective often lacking in anthropological studies about Morocco.

Cynthia Becker remarks in her introduction that "art, gender and ethnicity are the subject of this book." She gives primacy to the role that fertility and reproductive organs have in the comportment of Ayt Khabbash women and their artistic production and she emphasizes this role often by the repetitive use of some key words throughout the book. For the most part, she depicts marriage ritual in and around a village of the Tafilalet. Her book is solid when she describes those wedding ceremonies, the songs and dances around them, the brides' apparel and jewelry, and the customs that evolved around such events. The sole "artistic" activity described as being performed by the Ayt Khabbash women is that of weaving woolen mats and blankets, an activity on the brink of disappearance, as sedentary life replaces nomadic pastoral existence. This does not constitute and is far from constituting a rich study of Amazigh Arts in Morocco. The author added a seventh chapter to the book on Amazigh and non-Amazigh Moroccan painters, for the most part of the masculine gender; the addition does not actually extend her prior study of a local Amazigh feminine artistic production to a national or international level. The chapter also fails to point to the wealth and variety of Amazigh arts in Morocco and elsewhere in Berber land.

Cynthia argues at length that female fertility symbolism reigns throughout Amazigh arts. Such an argument is at best a limiting one. She does not situate the paucity of Ayt Khabbash textile production in the context of an overall richness of weavings coming out of the various regions of the Berber land of Morocco. Some rugs produced by Amazigh women in the Atlas Mountains have achieved the status of international 'art" in opposition to the simple local craft of making head coverings that she describes in the Tafilalet. She does not speak of the potters, or of the wood carvers, the metal workers, and the silver smiths that produce quality items throughout the Berber land of Morocco.

A few Moroccan studies of Amazigh traditions have detailed the formation of social categories in the region of the Tafilalet, based on the control of water rights and agricultural resources, and explained how various ethnic groups relate to the land and those resources. In such recent studies, one can learn how the Ait Khabbash themselves invaded the region by the end of the 19th century, confiscating most of the lands and property, and establishing pacts of protection ('tayessa") with local sedentary Arab groups. The more recent Arabization and Islamization of the whole region is minimized in Cynthia Becker's depiction which does not differentiate enough between Islamic practices and Amazigh traditions. One particular instance of such a lack of differentiation shocked me: weavings are said to have "soul" which is translated as "ruh": here the author seems to offer as a Berber word one that is actually an Arabic word right out of the Koran.

The region is also heavily inhabited by a group of Haratin people who constitute the near totality (around 80%) of agricultural labor. While Cynthia Becker devotes a portion of her book to a category of dark skinned people (Imskhan) who are considered descendants of former slaves from sub-Saharan regions, and have adopted ways similar to those of the Ayt Atta though they are Arabic speakers, she makes no mention whatsoever of the Haratin, a group of Saharan "free human beings" (Hrar) who speak Berber and are an important element of the population of the Tafilalet. They are simply inexistent in her book, a total cultural omission leaving a regrettable hole in the social tapestry she attempts to weave.

The book relates a personal and individual experience of a young American woman meeting with one aspect of the Amazigh world of Morocco, and it does that well. Given the scarcity of documentation on Amazigh life in the English language, it is an important testimony. Her central argument, however, that links the fertility power of Berber women to the maintenance of Amazigh ethnicity, though it surely has some validity, is over emphasized. She fails to analyze the extent of Islamic influence on dress, manners, and comportment of people living in an area known for its mixed culture. Finally, I expected far more on the topic of Amazigh arts in Morocco, and was disappointed by the absence of information on many aspects of our rich Amazigh artistic production in Morocco.

Published in International Journal of Middle East Studies, 2008 40:2 pp 341-342.

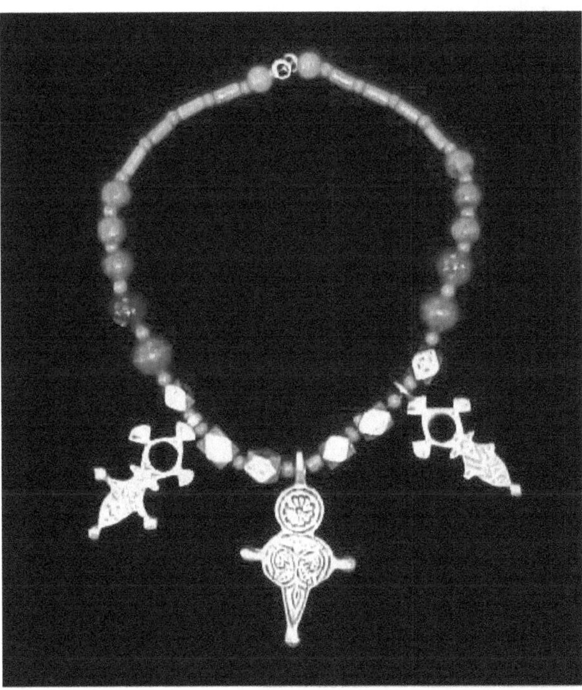

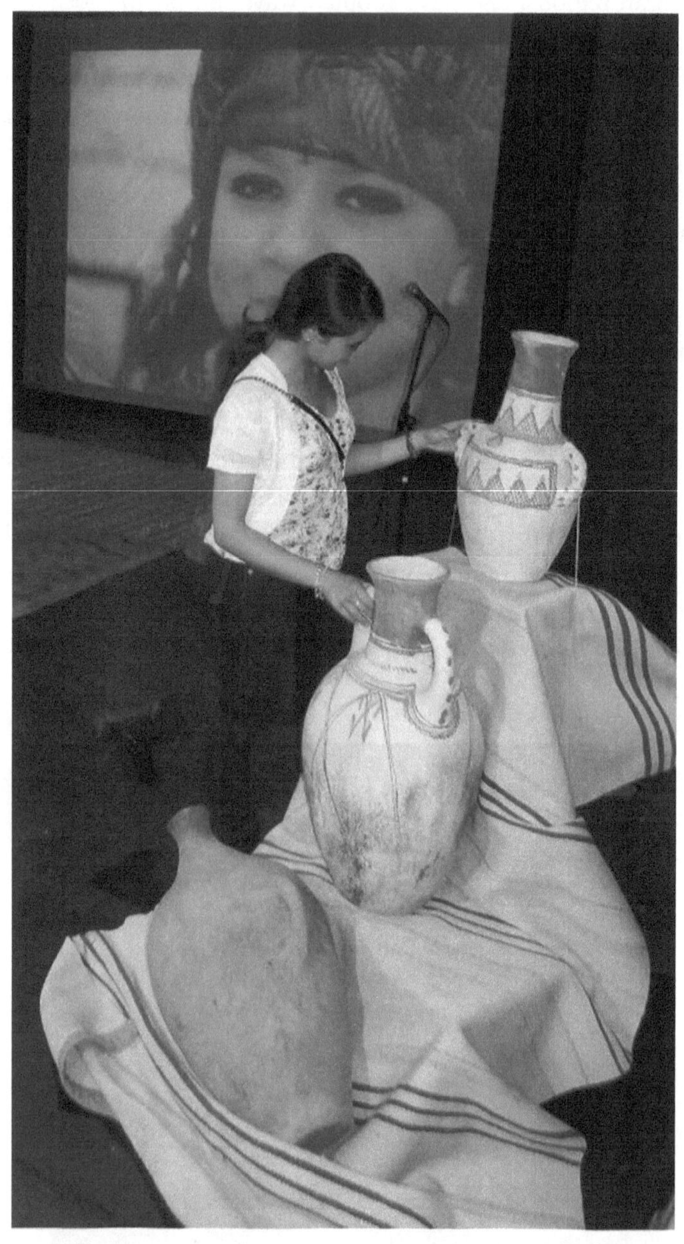

Young Amazigh of the Middle Atlas of Morocco, festival assistant, admiring pottery in Amazigh Art display at April 2012 Los Angeles Amazigh Film Festival. Pottery of the Rif, Amazigh blanket and rugs of High Atlas. Festival Director: Helene E. Hagan.

Book Review Three

"EVIDENCE FOR THE ANCESTORS OF THE GUANCHES AS FOUNDERS OF PREDYNASTIC EGYPT "– JONAH G. LISSNER

First, I need to underline that I am one of the few scholars who are of the opinion indeed that the founders of the Egyptian civilization belonged to one of the groups known as Libyans at the time, who inhabited the region west of the Nile Valley all the way to the Ocean Atlantic on the Moroccan coast. Those dwellers to the West of Egypt are known today as the Amazigh people (Berbers and Tuaregs.) In an Essay published in 2001, titled "The Shining Ones; Etymological Essay on the Amazigh Roots of Archaic Egyptian Civilization," I made and examined the proposition that the early founders of Egypt were possibly a group of proto-Amazigh people. Furthermore, during a television program aired in Los Angeles in 2003, I reviewed at length the relationship between the latest findings on Canarian mummification by a team of Canarian and British archeologists who brought out the similarities between Guanche and Egyptian mummies and a commonality of belief and symbolism, underlining how such findings added depth, and another dimension to my pioneer work.

It is from this perspective that I am reviewing the article written by Jonah Lissner. Until I read several pages of the piece that he wrote, I had not realized that he was a proponent of the white superiority of race, and it was not until he made a reference to Arthur Kemp, a white supremacist with bizarre theories, that I realized the motivation behind some of the statements made in his article. I was asked by Jonah Lissner to review his work, and I am doing so on his request.

The writer opens his remarks with a statement that the Guanches are "Nordic Caucasians." The Guanches of the Canary Islands were not of a monolithic ethnic descent. None of the information that we have about the Guanches who today consider themselves "Amazigh" actually reveals a Nordic origin or a Caucasian one. The most recent research on the early populations of North Africa to whom the Guanches seem to be related indicates a local development of a Cro-Magnon type, which has been distinguished from the "Caucasian" human ancestor of Europe, as well as the "Negroid" type of central Africa. Northwest Africa was peopled with a type known as "Mechtoid" (from Mekta site in Tunisia) which has been found in North Africa and along the coast of the Atlantic Ocean all the way to Mali. The evidence that we have is of two distinct Guanche racial types, one usually referred to as "Cro-Magnoid" and the other as "Mediterranean."

The second statement of Mr. Lissner concerning the Guanches is that they "dwelled in the Canary Isles, known as the Elysium, and the Garden of Hesperides by the classical Greeks….also known as the Fortunate Islands…" The Elysium was associated by the Greeks with the final resting place of blessed souls, a sort of Heaven, and was not determined to be any particular terrestrial abode, while the Garden of the Hesperides was indeed located in North Africa about the Atlas Mountains. The Hesperides were daughters of Atlas. To say that the Guanches resided in a heavenly abode of the imagination would be to deny their physical existence on earth, (fictitious characters, myth, and imaginary abode) and to place them in the Garden of the Hesperides is to locate them in the Atlas Mountains and not in the Canary Islands. There are very few references to that part of the world by Greek authors, and they are easy to examine. Despite assumptions and conjectures, none actually points to Elysium, the Garden of Hesperides, or the Fortunate Isles (Makaronesia) as being specifically the Canary Islands. Other candidates seem to be the ones designated. Strabo is the geographer quoted is this regard. But he wrote very clearly that the Fortunate Islands (Makarones) "lie west of the region where the end of Maurusia (Morocco) runs close to that of Iberia." Such islands would better designate the Azores. The Canary Islands lie west of the Western Sahara, and not west of the Detroit of Gibraltar.

Jonah Lissner then states that some of those Guanche people "sailed from the isles of West to found a new civilization in pre-dynastic Egypt at least 6,000 years ago." Such a statement is followed by the remark that the memory of this voyage is preserved in the later writings of Plato in his Timaeus. In the passage to which Lissner refers, Plato declares that there was once a large island (larger than Africa and Asia combined) beyond the straits of Gibraltar on which a dynasty of powerful kings arose that ruled all of Libya (Africa) to Egypt, and threatened to enslave all of the Mediterranean people, and that they were defeated. Not only were those rulers defeated by the early Greeks but their island – the Island of Atlantis - was swallowed by the sea and vanished from sight. Here, the Canary Islands are not only mistaken for a reference to the Azores, but they are assimilated to the mythical tale of a lost Atlantis. From that myth – and there is no historical evidence that such a tale is referring to actual events, or that such events involved the Canary Islands and their inhabitants the Guanches - Lissner establishes the basis for the foundation of the ancient Egyptian civilization. In my opinion, it is not warranted either by the Greeks geographers, historians, or even Greek myths.

However, the Greeks definitely placed the genealogy of Poseidon, the ruler of the seas, in that region, and they did locate the birth of a number of their important gods – borrowed from the Egyptians – in the land of Libya. The Kingdom of Tritonis (land which now lies east of Algeria and western Tunisia) was the birth land or cradle of all early arts and saw the passage from hunting gathering styles of life to agricultural settlements there. The domestication of the dog, the invention of the press to produce oil and wine, and the art of apiculture are attributed to a god/first human/teacher who walked the earth and taught mankind those skills, by the name of Aristaios. Aristaios was born and grew up in the kingdom or Tritonis situated on the continent of Africa, in what has always been and is now part of Tamazgha, ancestral Berber territory. The Greeks attributed to the Egyptians the knowledge of such origins, and respected that knowledge.

In regards to the Berber ancient Tifinagh alphabet, and Libyc inscriptions, there seems to be some confusion in Jonah Lissner's presentation. He writes: "It is known that their language closely resembles both Basque (Euskadi) and spoken Berber (the Tifinagh language), indicating an ancient or classical lingual and perhaps cultural linkage between the three groups….." Spoken Berber is not linguistically recognized as the Tifinagh language, but is called Tamazight. Some versions of this spoken language are the Tamashek of Tuareg speakers, the Tarifi of the Rif Mountains of Morocco, or the Tachelhit of the Souss Valley of Morocco. The ancient alphabet which left the written inscriptions of an earlier age to which Lissner refers to as Numidic or Punic inscriptions is the Tifinagh alphabet. Further in his recital, Lissner refers to the people of the Canary Islands as being "directly related to the ancient indigenous inhabitants of Northwest Africa, the Tamazight." The people are the <u>Amazigh</u> people of North Africa, or <u>Imazighen</u> (plural form) who speak <u>Tamazight</u> (Berber language.)

As to the role of Amazigh people in the history of Egypt, Lissner relies on a quote from Habiba Boumlik who is an anthropologist, well known to me as she is a member of the board of directors of the Tazzla Institute for Cultural Diversity which I founded and for which I have served as President since 1993. She is not a specialist in Egyptian history or culture. She made a simple and correct statement about Yennayer (New Year) and the Berber calendar, which was posted on the now defunct web site created by Bianca Madani. It refers to the reign of Sheshonq I and its significance for the Berber people of North Africa. This is a popular type of knowledge, and not a scholarly reference. Indeed, the "cross-cultural contacts" between Berbers and Egyptians which Lissner wants to illustrate, were far earlier and far more complicated that this simplistic reference obtained on the internet would indicate. Here, I must tarry a while and quote the author: "Concerning the evidence for cross-cultural contact between the northwest African Berbers and the Egyptians in remoter periods, in the classical period, circa 950-700 BCE, the Berber peoples had a reign of several pharaohs as cited by Habiba Boumlik: "the first mention of the Amazigh people in historical records:...."

The period of the reign of Sheshonq I and the Amazigh dynasty of Egypt to which Habiba Boumlik correctly refers was late, late Empire, and definitely not the classical period of Egyptian civilization, as Lissner would want his readers to believe. The mention of Tehenu and Tehemu (Amazigh Libyan groups and their chiefs) goes back to the earliest records of the Pyramid Texts, indeed the foundation era of Egyptian civilization, thousands of years earlier, and such references continued throughout the various dynasties. This quote by Lissner diminishes considerably the Amazigh roots of ancient Egyptian civilization while he is trying to prove the link between the Guanches (an Amazigh group, not a "Nordic" one) and early Egypt.

As I demonstrated in my book, "The Shining Ones, Etymological Essays on the Amazigh Roots of Ancient Egyptian Civilization, " numerous were the divinities of Egypt that were imported from Libya, or were essentially Libyan divinities of the desert, and those remained at the head of the developing of the Egyptian Pantheon of gods and goddesses. The primordial goddess Neith, revered by Egyptians as the mother of all gods, the protectress of the throne of the pharaohs and of all rulers of Egypt, was Libyan born, and considered imported from Libya. All rulers of Egypt were "her sons," sons of the bee which symbolized her. The entire complex of mummification and funeral rituals around the divinity of Osiris was maintained by a priesthood of Libyan origins, (Temple and oracle of Siwa) as were the all important ceremonies of coronation.

I am not comfortable at all with the premises advanced by Jonah Lissner concerning the foundation or roots of Egyptian civilization. My book relied on a large array of evidence provided by numerous archeologists with years of expertise in digs in the western region of Egypt, the desert of Libya, the Sahara and the Atlas Mountains of North Africa. It was grounded in such work. Etymological parallels were first scrutinized by Berber linguists, fluent in several regional Amazigh variations of Berber (Tashelhit, Tarifi, Tamazight, Kabyle, Tamashek) and not speculations on the part of European writers unfamiliar with Hamitic languages.

It is not until I reached past half of the article that I finally realized that some of the language which seemed peculiar belonged to a racist type of expression. Thus, when I came to a paragraph as the one I am going to quote, I could no longer evaluate this article as a serious objective enquiry. The racial bias seemed to skew all information:

"It furthermore does not emphasize the integral importance of the proto-Guanche donation of Pharaonic rulership; noting that a very high percentage of Egyptian rulers and pharaohs from the Pre-dynastic to the end of the New Kingdom were of Nordic stock and did not descend from the black-haired and fair-skinned or swarthy-skinned Mediterranean sub race, common to the Ancient Cretans. It was these hypothetical proto-Guanches from the West, led by Thoth, who brought with them a religion similar to that of the Nordic ruling elite of Lower Egypt."

Such verbiage is bound to leave any average reader incredulous. My book carefully unfolded the local development of traditions and religious ritual and did not speak of Nordic invasions and the import of Nordic stock and religion. I did not speak of a Nordic ruling elite of Lower Egypt, but on the contrary elegantly demonstrated how the symbols of rulership in Egypt emanated from the early pastoral economy of the Delta of the Nile and the Fayum region of the West of the Nile, and maintained those origins throughout centuries of historic existence. Historically, I also brought forward the irrefutable fact that the first Pharaohs of Egypt in 3,000 BC were preceded by a long ancestral line of fifty rulers known as "Libyan chiefs or princes," as the Palette of Palermo tells us.

Lissner writes of Caucasians, of a Nordic stock, and the inhabitants of a mythical Atlantis who were Aryans (whom he calls "proto Guanches") who sailed across the Straits of Gibraltar and landed by the mouth of the Nile where they created the Egyptian civilization. He writes: "Could it be the Pre-Dynastic founders of Egypt - Nordics or Mediterranean Caucasians – have been coming on the sails of the founders, their ancestors the Atlanteans –some thousands of years before, who built the Sphinx, Osireon, the Great Pyramid of Gizeh – which were later attributed to Khufu (circa 5000 years before present) – the racial descendant of the Amenti-dwellers of the west (i.e.post-Atlantean Cro-Magnon proto-Guanches)?"

My conclusions are inevitable: just as I am skeptical of Afro-centrist stories about the blackness of all civilization, I am skeptical of white Aryan stories about the Nordic white supremacy of all civilization. Either and both stir suspicion in me, and doubt. I have difficulty finding such scholarship acceptable. I consider such works as belonging to some sort of pseudo-scholarship, more akin to fiction than to history. Recent archeological studies have confirmed the North African and Saharan Amazigh origins of the Guanche population of the Canary Islands.

UCLA Lecture On Ancient Berbers

Originally published in "The Amazigh Voice", Volume 16, Issue 1, pages 13 and 14, Summer 2007

I recently received an invitation to attend a lecture titled "Ancient Berbers" which was sponsored by the African Studies Center of UCLA, University of California in Los Angeles, on April 27. I was definitely intrigued when I read the short paragraph promising "a new interpretation of the structures that supported the existence of ancient Berbers." The lecturer, Dr. Ramzi Rouighi, received his Ph D in History from Columbia University, and teaches Medieval and Modern Middle Eastern and African History at USC, University of Southern California, Los Angeles.

Dr. Rouighi opened his PowerPoint presentation with an apology about the fact that his research is ongoing and far from being completed, and that the theory he was about to introduce was the result of preliminary research. He then introduced the topic by stating that "Berbers" did not exist as such in ancient time, that there were no Berbers at the time Arabs invaded North Africa, and that the term "Berber" was a social category that emerged out of Andalusian history in medieval times around the ninth century.

With the help of archaic maps, Dr. Rouighi proceeded to demonstrate that the region of North Africa known today as the Maghreb was known to ancient historians under other names, and that the existence of "Berbers" was not recorded by those historians. The Greeks, he stated, used the word "Barbaroi" to describe many groups outside the Greek culture, and not necessarily and restrictively to designate the inhabitants of that region.

Indeed, he emphasized, the only part of a Ptolemaic map that contained the word "Barbaria" was located in Eastern Africa and not in North Africa.

When the Arabs invaded North Africa, they found Romans and Byzantines, continued Dr. Rouighi, and essentially the Arab conquest transferred the rule over the region from Romans to Arabs. At this point, having refrained from making any comments about the lack of information provided by Dr. Rouighi on a Berber presence from prehistoric to Roman times, I inquired of him what he made of the Treaty of Barca. In Arabic documents on the conquest of North Africa, the 643 AD Treaty of Barca in Cyrenaica (Libya) marks the first success of the invading forces over Berber forces, and the imposition of a war tax on Berber people, including several hundred heads of women and children in annual payment. (1) The Arabic record also indicates that this Treaty was a prototype for the treatment of other Berber groups brought into submission during the next few decades, from Libya to the Atlantic Ocean.

Dr. Rouighi stated that he did not know what I was talking about, had never heard of that treaty, but that he would get back to these matters later. He never did, of course. He went on, rapidly covering the period of the conquest of North Africa in a few words, passing almost immediately to a time and place more familiar to him, the medieval period of Al Andalus that followed the conquest of Iberia. In Iberia, according to him, ethnic identities were not immediately at issue. A Latin Chronicle covering the years 611-754 does not mention any "Berbers" but refers to people originating from Mauritania (referring of course to Mauritania Tinginita, the Roman province of what is now northern Morocco.) It was not until the 9th century AD in El Andalus that a social category of "Berbers" emerged to designate "the original inhabitants of the Maghreb," to differentiate them from "Arabs." The semantic term "Arab" itself, Dr. Rouighi affirmed, had a different meaning in the Iberian context that it had in the Middle East. To be an Arab in the world of El Andalus meant to be part of elite of Arabic descent.

Then, as he entered the domain of linguistics, someone in the room immediately asked whether Berbers spoke Arabic or another language, and I quickly made the comment that over thirty million people in North Africa speak Tamazight, or a form of Tamazight. I also mentioned that the very word "Berber" is a word alien to the vocabulary used by the original inhabitants of North Africa, who call themselves "Amazigh" (Plural "Imazighen") and that the word "Berber" is a label imposed by outsiders, and not a term of self-reference. A woman remarked that the period of history under study was the 9th century, and not the present, and I replied that the present only reflects continuity with the past under consideration. At that point, Dr. Rouighi skimmed over the linguistic question entirely to "summarize" and conclude the lecture.

In concluding, he brought out a quote from "The Berbers" by Brett and Fentress (previously reviewed by me, and part of this book.) The quote points to the numerous dialects spoken by the inhabitants of North Africa, sometimes incomprehensible to each other, and how difficult it is to refer to groups of people with disparate customs as a nation of Berbers. Similarly, he stressed, there were no Berbers in ancient times, let alone "proto-Berbers" in archaic times. The term "Berber" seems to be a semantic innovation introduced in Iberia in medieval times.

A black- skinned African American man remarked that when the Arabs invaded North Africa, they met people of his skin color, black Africans, and those were the Moors of medieval times. (2) Another African American man replied that it was useless to categorize people by skin color or other physical features, anyway, since we all come from Africa and differences are all human invention. Dr. Rouighi protested, however, that such a simplistic approach merely states that we all belong to the same humanity, but that the subject of History is precisely to investigate how human beings variously formulate ideas and convictions, and that this work is a valuable one.

In turn, I remarked that indeed statements as the quote he had selected point to the richness and diversity of elements pertaining to an Amazigh culture with ancient roots predating the arrival of Arabs in North Africa, and that the history of this culture has until now been mostly written by non-Amazigh historians, but this may not be the case in the future. (3) I added that the book titled "The Berbers" quoted by Dr. Rouighi is a very basic book, and that more sophisticated research has been conducted, for instance, by Dr. Malika Rachid and her team of anthropologists and archaeologists in Algeria, and couched in her remarkable book, "Les Premiers Berbères" (The First Berbers, Editions du Sud, 2001) In the near future, I added, more works written by Amazigh historians will be published. One is scheduled for publication in the United States in 2007. (4)

1.   In 642, under the rule of Caliph Umar I, an Arab general by the name of Amr Ibn Al As invaded Libya from Egypt, conquered the province of Cyrenaica, and established his headquarters in Barca. Despite the Treaty of Barca (643 AD), there was fierce resistance

in Tripolitania for years, broken by the forces of a subsequent invasion under Uqba Ibn Nafi. In his march across North Africa, Uqba Ibn Nafi applied the same rule of taxing each subdued group with a heavy war tax including an annual contingent of slaves as part of the booty.

2. It is a common fallacy among certain African Americans, sustained by revisionist History taught in Afro-centric schools, to proffer that the original inhabitants of North Africa were of Negroid stock. The record shows otherwise.

3. I did not mention my own book "The Shining Ones: Etymological Essay on the Amazigh Roots of Ancient Egyptian Civilization," XLibris, 2002.

4. "North African Mosaic: A Cultural Reappraisal of Ethnic and Religious Minorities", Nabil Boudraa and Joseph Krause Editors, Cambridge Scholars Publishing, July 1, 2007. My own review appeared on the back cover of the book:

"*North African Mosaic* is a significant landmark in the field of North African studies in the United States. In the past couple of decades, that field has primarily reflected the research and works of scholars in Near East or Islamic studies. It is therefore very satisfying to welcome the publication in the English language of a serious compilation of scholarly essays on North Africa which departs from such a monolithic perspective. The book offers an array of superbly informative essays on a variety of ethnic groups and issues, encompassing Amazigh (Berber) history, Amazigh arts, contemporary views on Amazigh identity and cultural survival, and a remarkable chapter on the peoples of the Western Sahara. Together, the depicted ethnic "minorities," Amazigh for the most part but not exclusively, constitute a majority of voices which have unfortunately often been overlooked in American universities and whose history and culture may no longer be ignored. *North African Mosaic* breaks stereotypes and the Arabo-Islamic lock on North African studies in America. The result is rich panoply of a little known contemporary North Africa. The perspective it offers its readers is not only refreshing, but undoubtedly more genuine in regards to the rich history and reality of a region which has not until now been examined in all of its diversity and effectively rooted in its African context."

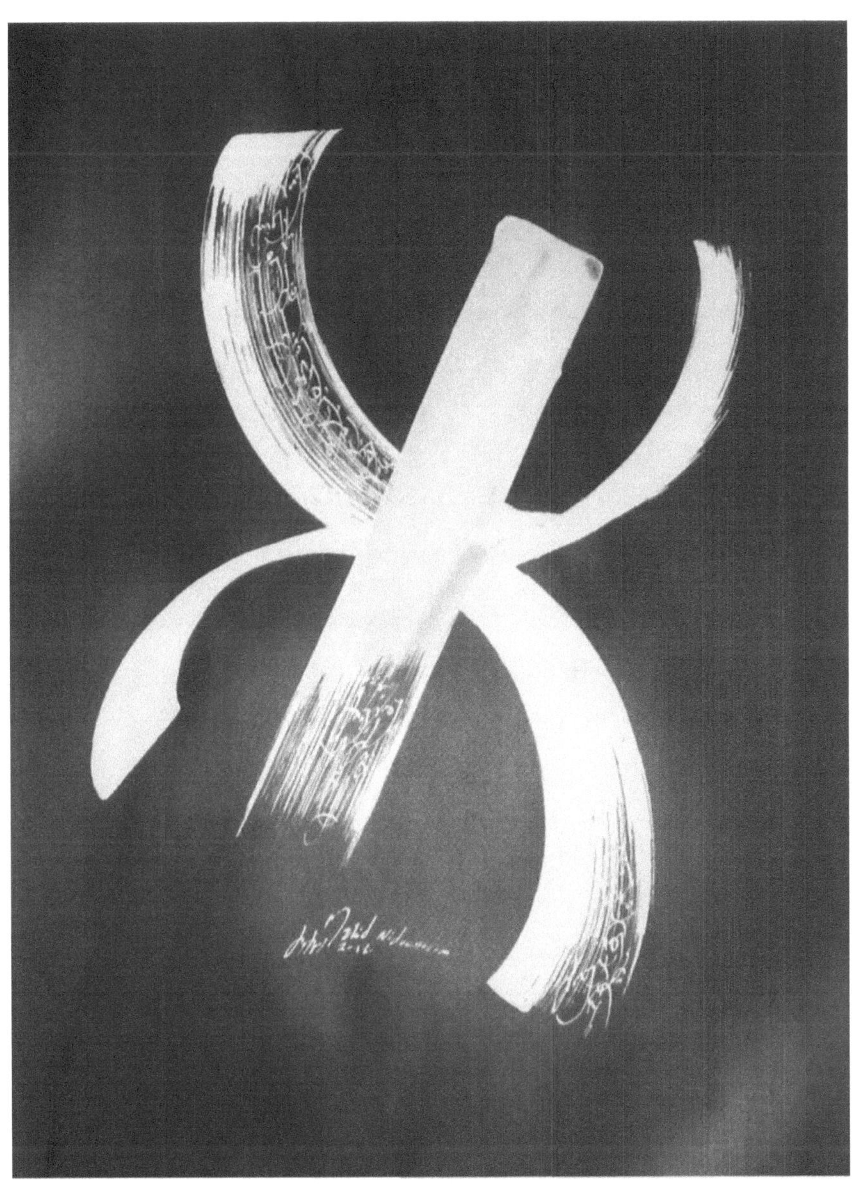

Artwork of Moulid Nidouissadan, Morocco

Amazigh Movement in Morocco

Re: Winter 2009, Volume 43 (2) PAGES 168-177 - "Ni Sauvage, ni Barbare, The Cultivation of "culture" in the Moroccan Amazigh Movement" by Paul Silverstein, Reed College.

Having just found this article on the internet, at the late date of February 2017, I am responding to Paul Silverstein's remarks on this Canadian/Moroccan documentary produced by Roger Cantin in 2008, and I am doing so for a number of substantial reasons. As the President of the Tazzla Institute for Cultural Diversity (1993-Present), I have consistently spoken and written to promote the Amazigh culture of North Africa, and that of Morocco more particularly. I was born and grew up in that land. Furthermore, because of my mother's Algerian judeo-berber origin, and because I was exposed to rural Berber traditions of Morocco in early childhood and adolescence, I selected Berbers of Morocco as a specialization for my doctoral anthropological studies at Stanford University. I became an activist in the Amazigh movement of Morocco some forty years ago and have never stopped supporting linguistic and cultural efforts on the part of Amazigh colleagues and activists. I am very familiar with this documentary which I presented to American audiences in January 2009 in Los Angeles, as a US Premiere of the Amazigh Film Festival I created in 2008, entering now its 9th annual year. The Tazzla Institute re-introduced it as well in 2010 at the United Nations of New York during a special annual event Tazzla Institute created and sponsored under the umbrella of UNESCO's Culture of Peace Program, which bears the name of "Creating Peace through the Arts."

The work of the Tazzla Institute for Cultural Diversity precedes the 1994 United Nations Convention which affirmed that "Cultural diversity is a cherished asset for the advancement and welfare of humanity at large and should be valued, enjoyed, genuinely accepted and embraced as a permanent feature which enriches our societies." It is my sincere hope that my response to the essay offered by Paul Silverstein on the cultivation of culture in the Moroccan Amazigh movement published in this journal of Middle East studies, regarding a documentary I personally selected nearly ten years ago to bring attention to the similarities of goals and means between Amerindian indigenous peoples and Amazigh autochthonous peoples of my native land, will be indeed well received by its academic readers.

Before I delve in the core issues raised by the Silverstein review, I would like to add to the background of my experience and achievement as a Moroccan Amazigh activist: I was instrumental in the selection of an American Indian activist to accompany me to the first international World Amazigh Conference that took place in Tafira, Grand Canary island, in August 1997. I sought Roberto Cruz, Papago activist of Arizona, a personal friend and Board member of the International Indian Treaty Council, for this role of mediation between cultures. He actually opened the Conference with a prayer in his native language, and conveyed to the assembly of Imazighen from various countries of North Africa the greetings and support of the American Indian Movement. At the same conference, I created a venue where this Indian activist could meet in private with Tuareg representatives of Mali and Niger in order to discuss matters of common interest in their struggles. At that meeting, I officiated as translator between Tuareg activists who spoke no English, but spoke French and Roberto Cruz who spoke no French but spoke English. Being fully bi-lingual in French and English, I was the intermediary in a long fruitful exchange between the two parties. Particularly moving was the translation of the poem recited by the great poet Hawad of Niger who opened the discussion on the Tuareg side. The similarities of viewpoints, of struggles, and of goals, were outlined and exchanged during several hours between Amerindians and North Africans.

Let me further present my profile as one of those Moroccan Amazigh activists targeted by Silverstein. I dedicated my entire professional life to American Indian and Amazigh issues, as a scholar and an activist, and created the Tazzla Institute to promote, protect and celebrate the Amazigh culture and Amazigh artists. I put together the first and only Amazigh Film Festival in the United States, and have presented the little known Amazigh (Berber and Tuareg) culture to Anglophone audiences of America for several years, in Los Angeles, New York and Boston. Selecting the documentary "Ni Sauvage, ni Barbare" was one of my first choices for this Amazigh Film Festival, as it was mentioned and recommended to me by no other than one of its protagonists, the Amazigh artist Lahbib Fouad (Yeschou) who leads the Berber side of this outstanding documentary. I liked the message it presented, which I knew to be a very poignant and valid one, given my own experience of the two cultures. It is relevant here to mention that I spent years on an Indian reservation, worked with the American Indian Movement and International Indian Treaty Council leaders, and created a very successful photo project with traditional Lakota elders, which I conceived and directed from 1983 to 1986 on the Pine Ridge Indian reservation of South Dakota. Upon my return to California, I opened an American Indian gallery, "Lakota Contemporary Designs" and was retained by the American Indian Alliance of Marin County to produce a community television series, "We are Still Here" featuring members of various Indian nations residing in that county. I then proceeded to create another series on the Amazigh culture of Morocco. The last two series I produced in Los Angeles were "Amazigh Weekly News" and "The Russell Means Show" in which I asked this famous American Indian activist, a close friend of mine, to host a number of half hour programs. In 2007, I was asked to present a week's segment on Amazigh Arts to a group of 20 or so professor/students during the first Berber Institute held at the Oregon State University, Corvallis, Oregon. Though my name is probably little known, I imagine, in the academic world of the United States, I have written numerous published articles and books on both cultures. If anyone has "cultivated" the culture of the Amazigh Movement in Morocco, as well as that of American Indians, I, among all anthropologists, scholars and activists, undoubtedly have.

'Ni Sauvage, ni Barbare" is the French title of this film. Paul Silverstein translates it as "Neither Savage, nor Barbaric" and even offers a quip by an unknown Moroccan (surely not an Amazigh activist?) as "Half Savage, half Barbaric." Silverstein simply omits, or appears to be unaware of the actual title for this documentary in English, which is "On Native Lands." As I write this analysis in English, I will continue to refer to the documentary by its correct name, "On Native Lands." Another item of vocabulary is also going to differ from the Silverstein review in my analysis: the plural form of Amazigh is "Imazighen." Wherever the term will be used to refer to Amazigh people in the plural form, the correct term of "Imazighen" will be used in this response to the Silverstein review.

"On Native Lands" gives a voice to an Amazigh artist and researcher at IRCAM (Royal Institute of Amazigh Studies, Rabat, Morocco), Lahbib Fouad, also known by the name of Yeschou, and an Innu singer, composer and activist from Labrador named Florent Vollant; through them, the film explores such issues as the marginalization of autochthonous peoples in North America and in North Africa, the question of cultural assimilation, the centrality of art in the maintenance of traditional values and in the grounding of identity. The respectful use of the environment is opposed to that of exploitation, and ritual links those notions. Silverstein advances that the protection of cultivated lands is claimed by groups who invoke their nomadic origins, and in doing so, he ignores the enormous diversity of lifestyles among Berbers or Imazighen of Morocco, from nomadic to semi-nomadic and sedentary ones; he also imputes the notion of "ethical stewardship of the environment" to colonial ethnologists, thereby concluding that the adoption of such claim is not only not new, but borrowed from colonial thinking. Here, I would like to disagree firmly and refer the readers of this article to my book "Tazz'unt, Ritual, Ecology and Social Order in the Tassaoute Valley of the High Atlas of Morocco" (2011) where I thoroughly review and discuss this matter with quotes from famous post-colonial anthropologists on the ancient practices of various tribal groups, from Papua New Guinea to the Amazon River, in regards to such ethical stewardship.

Silverstein sees in such attempts at survival on the part of autochthonous peoples the character of "self-primitivism" and makes the stupendous blunder of distinguishing Amazigh culture from Berber culture, as he asserts that the "underlying narrative" participates in what has been termed "the myth of the ecologically noble savage." He errs in doing so, as "Berber" has simply been an external appellation for peoples who have called themselves "Imazighen" (Singular "Amazigh") from the time of the pharaonic rulers of Egypt and before. The Amazigh culture is the ancient way of life of the peoples of North Africa whom outsiders have called "Berbers". Silverstein develops his review on the basis of this duality of perspective, Berber on one hand, and Amazigh on the other. And he concludes that "Berber and Amazigh cultures, whatever their overlap, prove to be distinct socio-political realities." The Tamazight language used in the central regions of Morocco and the Tamasheq language which is used by the Tuaregs of the Sahara desert both reflect what is evident throughout the North African territory called "Tamazgha" by autochthonous peoples, that the millennia old traditions of that land do belong to the peoples who have for centuries called themselves Amazigh/Imazighen. In my first book published in 2001, titled "The Shining Ones: Etymological Essay on the Amazigh Roots of Ancient Egyptian Civilization", I clearly define the Egyptian understanding of the land of "Tamazgha" as land ("Ta") of the Mazices ("Mazigh") or Libyan people who dwelt from the west bank of the Nile to the Atlantic Ocean. The expression "Tamaz-ra" in archaic Egyptian hieroglyphs refers to those who are sun-worshippers, who adore the sun, and they are said to be the peoples who inhabit the territory west of the Nile called Libya. Present day Berber people are firmly rejecting the external label put on them in a pejorative way, one of "Barbaric" people, and have re-affirmed their own ancestral name of Amazigh. The distinction which Silverstein proposes in his argument as he invents two different "socio-political realities" of Berber and Amazigh cultures, is not factual, and only serves a spurious narrative.

What is remarkably absent from that narrative and all of Silverstein's analysis is the spiritual dimension present in the discourse of both the Innu singer and the Amazigh artist and their families. It is this element which links them, indeed which links all the components of the film, from the stones carefully selected for the sweat-lodge ritual to the artwork and the songs shared between the cultural representatives of the two continents. Such a perspective was not particularly held, as Silverstein suggests, by "colonial anthropology" but rather brought forth in a fairly recent past by post colonial anthropologists. The "structural nostalgia" which he notes exists only in his mind, and not in the realities of space and time as understood and lived by earth peoples, Imazighen of North Africa and the Sahara desert, and the Innu people. Silverstein writes: "Such a self-primitivising visions of Berber nature and culture informs explicit enactments of Berber politics." Grammatically incorrect (a vision informs, or visions inform would have been correct English), this statement is also ludicrous. Here the argument of "self-primitivism" totally ignores the power of art, ritual, poetry and language in the creation and maintenance of any ethnic identity which struggles to survive in the face of colossal forces seeking its eradication. Silverstein indeed does not address the issue of identity, which is the central formidable issue common to all marginalized autochthonous groups of the world. In the film, one of my friends, one of the leading Amazigh activists of Morocco, head of Tamaynut, an Amazigh association which has over 30 branches throughout Morocco, and at one point representative of all African autochthonous groups at the United Nations Forum on Indigenous Peoples (IPACC), Hassan Id Belkhassam clearly states: "Autochthonous peoples throughout the world are denied their lands, their resources, their identity."

The review pursues in raising the question of the place of Harratin among Imazighen, whom Silverstein represents by the color of their skin, "black", and not by their known ethnic origins and social status among Imazighen. This is serious, as the imputation of racism is invoked in Silverstein's review. As I wrote in an essay published in "Fifty Years in America, Anthropological essays" (2013), titled "Islam and the enslavement of Africans":

"The Harratin have mysterious origins, which scholars have long debated. They are more closely related, genetically, to the Berbers of North Africa than to Black Africans, and yet they are a black-skinned population. Some scholars have seen in them the direct descendants of the original prehistoric inhabitants of the Sahara. They once worked in the oases of the desert as serfs or domestic servants of the Tuaregs, and considered themselves closely allied to them, forming a class category, which was not equated by Arabs or Tuaregs with that of slaves.

Indeed, the Arabic word for slave is "Abd," a word not applied to Harratin people. At the time Moulay Ismail gathered his elite black troops (14th century,) his general El Bakhri conscripted some Harratin, to the outcry of the Scholars of Fez and of the general population of Morocco, creating a great stir in the country, as Harratin were considered to be "Free Men" or "Imazighen" not subject to a conscription of black slaves."

Under a paragraph titled "Inequity", Silverstein falsifies history to accuse Amazigh people - Imazighen - of having bought Harratin slaves for their own purposes. Such an assertion distorts the truth of the trans Saharan slave trade. Some time before the 2001 World Conference Against Racism, Racial Discrimination, Xenophobia and Related Intolerance that took place in Durban, South Africa, I was delegated the task of researching and writing a special paper for the World Amazigh Congress, whose representatives were concerned that some sub-Saharan participants were planning to accuse Arabs and Berbers lumped into one group of conducting the large trans Saharan Slave Trade. A short version of the report I wrote after months of intensive research at the UCLA Library, both in French and in English, appears in the book I published in 2013, "Fifty Years in America" and in this book, under the title "Islam and the Enslavement of Africans", with an extensive bibliography on the subject matter. My research amply documents the facts that this slave trade began with and benefited the Arab invaders of Africa, and only became a source of income for the Berber tribes along the northern borders of the Sahara desert as they became stations between the North African coastal territory and the sub-Saharan slave depots. The caravans transporting black slaves to markets situated along the littoral of the Mediterranean Sea, to be sold to Arabs of Egypt and the Peninsula of Arabia, crossed Berber territory and were taxed consequently by Berber groups. As for the Tuareg groups of the Sahara Desert, to whom Harratin were attached in a feudal system, they were paid handsomely to protect those caravans as they crossed the desert. Enormous funds were needed to equip the costly caravans of the Arabic slave trade, and those were provided by Jewish bankers established in Italy, Spain and northern Africa. Some Berber groups were paid for allowing the trade to pass through their territory and establish rest stops, while Tuaregs were solicited as a police force to protect the safety of the voyagers, demanding substantial remuneration. Often, both Berbers and Tuaregs were paid in goods and slaves. Given those verifiable facts in the history of the slave trade conducted by Arabs in Africa, it is no wonder that Amazigh people would object to the misconceptions of events in Silverstein's review which accused them of "racial exclusion" toward a group of their own "free" people, the Harratin.

The Silverstein review of the Roger Cantin' documentary "On Native Lands" introduces a duality between Berber and Amazigh cultures which does not exist, misrepresents the struggle for identity among indigenous peoples of North America and North Africa, and accuses the autochthonous peoples of Morocco of creating social categories based on skin color, a distinction which might be factual in American society, but not real in a region of Africa where the skin color of "free people" (Imazighen) ranges from very light to very dark, passing through all the hues of tan, coffee, bronze, red and ebony known to mankind, and where skin color does not determine social status, except among the alabaster white skinned Arabic invaders who deemed inferior to them all other non-white human beings. Brandishing sword and a book holy to them, these invaders of North Africa were the instigators and the recipients of a slave trade which started first in North Africa, enslaving large numbers of Amazigh people in Libya, Tunisia, Algeria and Morocco, boys and girls shipped to the Middle East in lieu of exorbitant war tax payments, a lucrative trade which later, as early as the 8th century, crossed the Sahara Desert in search of black slaves. The fundamental arguments advanced by Silverstein in this review, that Amerindians and Imazighen resort to an obsolete notion of a "Noble savage" for political purposes, and that a newly acquired Amazigh respect for Jewish ways serves to humanize the image of Barbarian people who aspire to a certain modernity incarnated, according to him, in the symbol of the Jew, are altogether untenable, unfounded, misleading, and injurious.

Bibliography:

Hagan, Helene E. : "Tazz'unt, Ritual, Ecology, and Social Order in the Tassaoute Valley of the High Atlas Of Morocco." (XLibris, 1911)

Hagan, Helene E.: Bibliography, "Islam and the Enslavement of Africans." in "Fifty Years in America, Essays" (XLibris, 1913)

Hagan, Helene E.: The Amazigh International Network, United Nations Pipe Conference (Indigenous People and the Environment) 2001, in "Fifty Years in America, Essays" (XLibris, 1913)

Helene E. Hagan - Black Elk Peak, Black Hills, South Dakota (1987)

FRENCH INDIANS OF AMERICA

The Neglected Story of French-Indian Unions in Early America

"L'histoire du peuple métis et de ses combats pour la défense de son idéal de société est un héritage qui n'a pas fini de nous inspirer." Gilles Havard (Histoire de l'Amérique Française, 2008)

In modern history, the British language prevailed in the United States of America, where heroes of Anglo Saxon origins are generally recalled while the memory of the extraordinary adventures of thousands of French and French Canadian explorers, instrumental in the discovery of the North American continent south of the Great Lakes, is no longer cultivated, sometimes erased, and seldom invoked and remembered.

Who even knows today, for instance, that the legendary Davy Crockett who died at the Alamo in 1836 was of French ancestry? He was born David de Crocketagne in 1786 in Tennessee, the descendant of a French Protestant refugee. Who has even heard of Nicolas Perrot (1665-1689), French explorer, "coureur des bois". interpreter, and diplomat in the region of the Great Lakes? And yet, together with other Frenchmen Toussaint Baudry and Jean Desroches, he was the first French trader to deal with the Algonquin tribes near Green Bay, Wisconsin. He was to become a very important mediator between Indians and French in the Upper Mississippi where he established three forts. In 1689, as representative of the King of France at Fort Saint Antoine, he formally claimed possession of all the Upper Mississippi and the country of the Sioux. His Memoirs on *The Indian Tribes of all the Upper Mississippi and the Region of the Great Lakes* (1680-1718) is a precious document of early Aboriginal life. Has anyone even heard of French military man and explorer Louis Armand, Baron of Lahontan (1666-1715), whom some historians recognize as having first reached the Missouri River (French name of Longue Rivière)? Who today remembers the young exploits of Jean Vincent Baron de Saint-Castin, (1652-1707), a French officer who became headman of a Penobscot Indian tribe (Acadia/Maine) in which he had married?

There is a general amnesia in the narratives of the American frontier concerning the two centuries of a vibrant French colony ranging from the eastern seaboard to the Rocky Mountains, the rich French heritage of the region of the Great Lakes and the early French colonization of the vast Louisiane territory which encompassed the region of the Great Plains. So little is taught in American history of the enormous work and cultural impact of French and French Canadian missionaries, "voyageurs", and intrepid young men who actually founded America; they were the first Europeans to encounter groups of Aboriginal peoples of North America, trade with them, marry their women and live with them, and to ultimately engender a large new ethnic group of mixed breeds, the métis French-Indian children and their descendants who built the solid foundations of the American nation. The record indicates that thirty one states of the United States were discovered, explored or colonized by Frenchmen.

Written with a small "m", the word "métis" is an old French word which signifies "mixed" and the French verb "métisser" means "to crossbreed". "Métissage" is the word used in France for mixed ancestry. The term was first used for people of dual Indian and white ancestries. When capitalized, "Métis" became the designation of a specific ethnic group, the Métis Nation of Canada. In the United States, the name of métis would apply generally to offspring born to indigenous women and Frenchmen in Nouvelle France, the Great Lakes region, and the original territory of Louisiane. which included eleven present-day states, Louisiana, Arkansas, Kansas, Missouri, Montana, North and South Dakota, Nebraska, Oklahoma and parts of Minnesota and Texas. France indeed was the first European nation to hold any claim to South Dakota.

People of mixed ancestry (excluding the Métis Nation of Canada) were the offspring of unions which began on the eastern seaboard of America, and spread westward as French "voyageurs," "coureurs des bois", interpreters, as well as employees of the fur trading Hudson Bay company and garrison troops of the Great Lakes area and the vast Louisiane Territory, married young Indian women in "the fashion of the country" ("a la façon du pays"), that is without the benefit of civil or religious ceremonies. Such unions, even though considered illegal, and unacceptable to the Jesuits and the Catholic Church, often lasted for life. Native women often converted to protect their marriage and the status of their children.

Historical literature in English on the arrival of these early French individuals in the Great Plains is sparse. Both in the United States and in Canada, substantial writings in English refer only slightly to this early segment of pioneers in the Plains. There has not been a great recognition of the French presence. Thus, the Encyclopedia of the Great Plains, published in 2003, admits:

"Lack of familiarity with the language of that minority hampers western historians access to the French-speaking part of the history of the Plains."

Indeed the history of French-Indian relations is a legacy which has not been fully narrated by American historians and needs to be recognized and honored. The language of the fur trade in America was French. The first explorers of the region known as Nouvelle France in Canada, the Haut Pays (upper region) and Bas Pays (lower region) and the vast territory of Louisiane originally claimed by the French around the Great Lakes, and along the Mississippi and Missouri Rivers, were Frenchmen and French Canadians who played a very important role in the expansion of the French influence in North America.

For almost three centuries, French wood runners, fur trappers and fur traders were the first Europeans who penetrated dense forests and navigated waterways, a unique adventure in the overall history of America. This is for the most part a neglected, if not forgotten, America and a history of an era preceding the conquest of the West, that of Europeans - for the most part French - in search of pelts and encountering autochthonous peoples. These were young adventurous men who mingled with indigenous tribes, learned their languages, married their daughters, and gave birth to a new ethnic group of French Indian offspring.

Their travels ranged from South Carolina to the Mississippi, from the Valley of the Saint Lawrence to the Rocky Mountains. In his "Histoire des Coureurs des Bois", French author Gilles Havard wrote : "With their Amerindian spouses, White French Indians and their descendants populated the vast stretches of prairies where the buffalo reigned." (Histoire de l'Amérique française, Gilles Havard and Cécile Vidal, 2008).

Another French author, Jacques Bodelle, has recently outlined an extensive French presence in the United States in "Petites Histoires des Français d'Amérique", (Editions Mélibée, 2014), lamenting the paucity of information on this topic in the English language. Though his contribution is notable, this author also omits much of the French and Indian relations in the Plains in this particular book, an omission I personally discussed with him. I found his essay written in 2005 and published in the Sabix Bulletin 38, pages 5-27, titled "Those Frenchmen who made America" (Ces Français qui ont fait l'Amérique) far more interesting in this regard. He opens the essay with this remark:

> *"Four hundred thousands at least, perhaps half a million, is the number of French people living in the United States today. This number would be far greater, six or seven million, if it took into account individuals of French descent, of long ago or more recent, who do not always remember the origin of their surnames or their origins at all."*

Jacques Bodelle also observes that the heart of the continent was originally French and would remain French until the dawn of the nineteenth century. He retraces the voyages of a number of French explorers, from the early missions of French Jesuits to the Lewis and Clark Expedition of 1803 which had to rely on a French trapper, Toussaint Charbonneau and his Shoshone wife Sacagawea for guidance throughout the three years of that exploration.

In order to illustrate and shed some light on the magnitude of the French presence of that era, this chapter will (summarily, I must admit) outline, step by step, the role of the Franciscan Récollet and Jesuit missions in making first contacts with aboriginal groups, the establishment and expansion of the French fur trade (1534-1763) from the St Lawrence Valley of Nouvelle France to the Plains, and the French military forts of the Dakota and the Nebraska Territories which occasioned the birth of thousands of French Indian offspring in that specific region of America.

The Missionaries

The very first act of trade between Europeans and Amerindians took place when French navigator Jacques Cartier encountered some Micmac Indians on July 7, 1534. His explorations of the St Lawrence River led to the claim of Canadian land by France. In Canada, the Jesuits began their missionary work among the Hurons in 1634. Before that, Samuel de Champlain, the first governor of New France, had spent the winter of 1615-1616 with a group of Hurons. He was the first explorer to use the disparaging name of "Huron" to refer to the Wendat people, a more correct appellation which rarely occurred in the texts of the *Jesuit Relations*. De Champlain returned in 1623 in the company of Joseph Le Caron, a Récollet Franciscan Friar and two other Récollets, Franciscan Father Nicolas Viel and Brother Gabriel Sagard-Théodat. They met with Hurons during the winter of 1623-1624.

It is the narratives of the *"Jesuit Relations"*, begun in missionary work from those early years which left posterity with a record of those encounters.

At this juncture, it is important to note that letters and other documents edited by Pierre Margry (1818-1894), French Archivist and Historian, Director of Navy and Colonies, Paris, France, during years of meticulous research and which are stored in the Bibliothèque Nationale of France, have thrown a flood of light upon early French discoveries and explorations, especially on the travels of La Salle in America. Several volumes were published as «Découvertes et établissements des Français dans l'Ouest et dans le Sud de l'Amérique...» in 1879. In the United States, Francis Parkman (1823-1893) worked closely with Margry to retrieve those early documents and make them available to American historians.

For the Jesuits, Indian Territory represented the "pays des nations alliées" (country of allied nations), "pays des Sauvages éloignés de la colonie française" (country of faraway Savages of the French colony) and "Pays des Beufs" (Country of the Bison, the Great Plains, so designated by Récollet Father Louis Hennepin, an early explorer of Minnesota). In regards to the Sioux people in particular, the French Jesuits in their letters divided them into two categories: "Les Sioux des Bois" (The Sioux of the woods, Dakotas or Santees) and "Les Sioux des Prairies" (The Prairie Sioux, Nakotas and Lakotas).

The Merchants and the French fur trade

A merchant named Pierre de Chauvin acquired the rights of Canadian fur trading in 1599, granted by Henri IV, King of France. In 1614, Champlain created the Company of Merchants for Rouen and Saint Malo. A few years later, the monopoly of this trade was assumed by another Frenchman, Aymar de Chaste. Founded in 1642, Montreal became the center of fur trading, while three secondary trading posts were soon established on the St Lawrence River banks, Tadoussac, Trois Rivières, and Sorel. The first agents who lived and traded with Huron and Montagnais Indians were Jean Nicollet, Etienne Brulé and Nicolas Marsolet. Nicolas Marsolet de Saint Aignan lived a long life (1587-1677), trading for 27 years with the Montagnais people, acquiring the surname of "Little King of Tadoussac" and serving as an interpreter of the Montagnais and Algonquin languages. He was remembered as a venturesome, courageous man, rugged in his ways, and spirited, a true legend of the early days of the Canadian fur trade. Jean Nicollet took for wife a woman of the Huron nation, with whom he had a daughter. Etienne Brulé served as pathfinder, scout and interpreter, and was the first European to explore what is now the state of Pennsylvania. Accused of treachery, he was killed by the Hurons.

Louis Jolliet and Jacques Marquette began exploring the Mississippi which at the time was called "Mesuji" (The Great Water) or also "ne tango" (Big River). The French referred to that river as "Fleuve Colbert." Jolliet's expedition had been commissioned by Louis de Frontenac, Governor of New France. He and Marquette travelled with five métis "voyageurs" of French Indian ancestry. An expert in the Huron language, Jesuit Jacques Marquette was fluent in six different American Indian languages. He was the founder of Sault St. Marie, the first European settlement of Michigan. The fur trade of Nouvelle France enticed thousands of young Frenchmen to navigate into unknown territory in search of a variety of pelts, the commerce of beaver fur being the most lucrative of all. In 1626, Jesuit Charles d'Allement wrote that the furs traded were: "moose, lynx, fox, badger and muskrat, but they deal principally in beavers for greatest profit."

There were "voyageurs" of the legitimate fur companies, "coureur des bois" who were independent fur trappers and traders with Indian trappers, and later the "engagés", paid employees under three-months contracts of large fur trading enterprises, working in trading posts or navigating canoes on rivers. The fur trade had immense and complex consequences of social, political and economic dimensions. It was essential to the forging of alliances with numerous Indian tribes, and also caused rivalries between them for access to prized trade items, from metal objects, beads and textiles to alcohol and guns. The trade introduced devastating diseases among Indians, and led to conflict and war between British, French and their respective indigenous allies.

In Louisiane, French explorer René-Robert Cavelier de la Salle navigated the Big River (Mississippi) to its mouth, and two brothers, Pierre and Jean-Baptiste Le Moyne d'Iberville et de Bienville built the region, founding Fort Maurepas, Fort La Boulaye, and Fort Saint Louis. The territory of Louisiane dates back to 1702. New Orleans was founded in 1718 by younger brother de Bienville, who developed a vast colony and rightfully acquired the name of "Father of Louisiana." Their own father was Charles LeMoyne de Longueil (1626-1685), a Frenchman who migrated to Canada in 1641 and became a fur trader.

Dakota Territory

The first European to enter North Dakota was a fur trader, a Frenchman by the name of Pierre de la Verendrye who explored the upper Missouri and Mandan country. In 1739, Pierre de la Vérendrye and Paul Mallet are the first Europeans to reach a mountain range near the source of the Platte River. Pierre Gaultier de Varennes de la Vérendrye (1685-1749) was a French Canadian soldier, fur trader and explorer, one of the greatest explorers of the west. In the fall of 1938, La Verendrye reached an Indian village on the Missouri, near what is present day Bismark, North Dakota. With his two sons, François and Louis Joseph, he later pushed further, reaching the Black Hills of South Dakota, claiming the entire Dakota Territory for France. They established Fort Saint Pierre in 1727, Fort St Charles in 1732, Fort Dauphin in 1741 and Fort La Reine in 1738. A tablet commemorating their expedition was placed on a hill overlooking the present-day capital of South Dakota, Pierre, on March

30, 1743. This tablet documents the brothers Vérendrye as the first known French explorers on the northern plains. It was not until 1817 that an American Fur Trading post was established in Fort Pierre.

Built in 1832, Fort Pierre Chouteau, the center of trade for the American Fur Company, became one of the most important fur trade forts of the western frontier. It was established by Pierre Chouteau (1789-1865), a member of the wealthy Chouteau family of St. Louis. It was at Fort La Framboise, Fort Tecumseh and Fort Pierre that the bulk of the fur trade of the Northwest took place for over forty years. Fort Tecumseh was built in 1822 by the Columbia Fur Company.

Fort La Framboise was established in 1817 on the south side at the mouth of the Bad River by a voyageur named Joseph Francis La Framboise. La Framboise came from one of the earliest French families to settle in Canada. Its patriarch was originally named Bertrand Fafard; he acquired the nickname of Framboise (Raspberry). His descendant, Joseph Francis La Framboise is associated with the earliest settlement of South Dakota. He was a mixed-breed Indian man, whose mother, Madeline Marcotte, was a half Ottawa Indian. Widowed, she became a competent and wealthy manager of several trading posts for the American Fur Company at age 50. Her grand father was Ottawa Chief Kewinoquot. At age 14, Madeline married Joseph La Framboise. Madame La Framboise (1780-1846) was a great asset to her husband in the fur trade. She was a métis, a French-Indian woman. Her son also became a fur trader who in 1827 married Magdeleine Sleepy Eyes, a Sisseton Sioux, after the death of his first wife, a daughter of Walking Day, a Sioux headman. In later years, La Framboise moved to Flandreau where he opened another fur post.

Nebraska Territory

Fort Laramie, originally established as a private fur trade post in 1834 evolved into a large military post before it was abandoned in 1890. In 1834, Lucien Fontenelle reports the completion of the fort to Pierre Chouteau Jr. of the American Fur Company. The following year, in 1835, 2,000 Oglala Indians brought skins, moccasins and pelts to exchange for knives, awls, combs, metal pots, etc... For some fifty six years it served as a prominent center and capital of a lucrative fur trade empire for successive generations of trappers, traders, American Indians and garrison troops. It was named after one of the French Canadian beaver hunters who were the first men of European origin to explore the headwaters of the North Platte River. The man was Jacques Laramee or Laramie, killed by Arapaho Indians near the river. Among the early fur traders of the Fort Laramie region was François Antoine Larocque who traded furs on the Powder River in 1805.

The French knew of the Otoe and Missouri Tribes in Nebraska as early as 1673. It was the date at which Father Marquette mapped Nebraska, quite accurately, identifying the tribes he had met there as Omaha, Pawnee and Otoe. The name "Nebraska" was taken from the Otoe word "Nebrathka" meaning "flat water." The Platte River was named after the French word for "flat." For more than a century prior to 1763, the Upper Missouri river, including what is today the Badlands National Monument, was under French control. The early French Canadian trappers called the region "Les Mauvaises Terres a Traverser" (The bad lands to travel across). The Dakota Indians called the region "Mako sica" (Bad Land).

In 1714, French explorer Etienne Veniard, Sieur de Bourgmont reached the Platte River. In 1824, Jean-Pierre Cabanné began to operate a trading post north of Omaha, the Cabanné Trading Post, at the confluence of Ponca Creek and the Missouri River. The French posts in Nebraska also included the Bordeaux Trading Post, the Post of the Otoes and the Robideaux Pass Trading Post. Susan Bordeaux Bettelyoun (1857-1945), born to fur trader James Bordeaux and Huntkalutawin, a Brule Lakota woman, left a written record of those trading days.

The first town of Nebraska was established by French people, south of Ohama. It was the Fontenelle's Post built in 1872 in the Nebraska Territory, later site of the city that was called "Bellevue." The Fontenelle Post served as a center for trading with Omaha, Otoe, Missouri and Pawnee tribes. Lucien Fontenelle, born in 1800 into a wealthy French Creole family of New Orleans, married a Native American woman by the name of "Bright Star" or "Bright Sun." She began to live with him in 1824. She was the daughter of an Omaha headman named Big Elk. Fontenelle operated in Sarpy County, eastern Nebraska from 1822 to 1832. The Omaha (as well as the Osage) observed a patrilineal system of descent. Therefore, the children of mixed marriages with Frenchmen had no status among them, and the five children of that union had an European education. Lucien Fontenelle was named US Indian Agent at Fort Laramie where he died.

The town of Chadron - in Lakota "beaver river city" - was named in honor of Louis Baptiste Chartran (1795-1854), a French Indian Métis trapper, son of Jean-Baptiste Chartran and Marguerite Desrosiers. He was an accomplished trader and interpreter, married to the daughter of Bull Tail, a Brule Sioux. In 1841, they were operating a fur trading post on the Bordeaux Creek. Their son George, born in 1848, spent his life on the Rosebud Reservation under the name of Plenty Horses.

The town of Bordeaux was named after Pierre Bordeaux, a French trapper and trader who originally came from the city of Bordeaux, France. Pierre Bordeaux was a fur trader operating in northwestern Nebraska from 1830 to 1870.

The town of Barada was named after Antoine Barada, son of French trapper and interpreter Michel C. Barada. It was located in the Nemaha Half-Breed Reservation or Tract which was of short duration (1830-1860). The Half-Breed Tract was established by Article 10 of the Treaty of Prairie du Chien of 1830, to provide land for those mixed-breed Indians who did not quite fit either in white American society or in Indian society, looked upon as "social orphans." In 1833 about 200 half-breeds resided in the Tract. They were listed in 1857 as descendants of Otoe, Iowa, Omaha, Yankton and Santee Sioux. Out of a number of 445 that year, 185 were listed as Yankton half-breed Indians. The half-breed reservation was legally terminated in 1860.

Joseph Deroin (1819-1858) was the son of a Métis French Canadian trapper, Amable de Rouin and his Otoe wife who had traded along the Missouri River for decades. In 1840, Joseph Deroin set up a trading post at the mouth of the Platte River. He married an Omaha Indian woman, and in 1842 two Métis sisters, Julia and Susée Baskette, daughters of an Otoe Indian woman. American settlers gradually invaded the Tract and built around the Deroin's post which was engulfed in the white settlement, now the town with the name of St. Deroin.

Frenchmen married Native women for a number of reasons, not the least ones being economic reasons. Besides the obvious reason that there was a scarcity of European women available to voyageurs et coureurs des bois in unexplored territories, marriage to important headmen led to alliances with Indian groups, better treatment and better trade. Moreover, Indian wives constituted a real asset in the fur trade, as they tanned skins, and learned French, often serving as interpreters. At the rendez-vous or on hunts, women were essential to the operation of the fur trade. They made the moccasins, the snowshoes, the birch bark canoes and other equipment essential for travel on winter hunts. In the Plains, where the principal item of trade became the buffalo hides, native women prepared the bison robes as well as beaver and otter pelts for clothing.

During the early years of fur trade expansion, intermarriages between French traders and Indian women occurred in a tribal setting. As native wives began to move to trading posts and forts, customary marriage - initially a non legal form of marriage without the benefit of civil or religious sanction - became lawful. Between 1785 and 1830, the majority of children born in fur trading posts were born of French fathers and Indian mothers, or from Métis-Indian intermarriages and métis-métis unions. By 1800, women of mixed descent replaced native women as spouses of choice, as their number increased. Entire communities of mixed breeds began to form. While in Canada a new ethnic group of mixed breeds invoked a language of their own, Mitif, and an identity of their own, that of Métis, in the United States, the situation differed. After 1820, the American métis identity disappeared as government policies categorized people as either "native" or "white", with no specific classification for individuals of mixed descent. The end of the country marriage as an institution came about 1830 with the decline of trade with Indians.

Fort Laramie - Painting by Alfred Jacob Miller

GLOSSARY for French Indians

- *Alfred Jacob Miller* (1810-1874) : artist employed by Sir William Stewart to document an expedition of 1837. His paintings are the only artistic documents of the fur trade created by someone who actually took part in it. The American Heritage Center at the University of Wyoming in Laramie holds several original paintings by A.J. Miller.

- *"Black Robes"*: name given by Native Americans to the three groups of Catholic missionaries, the Franciscan Récollets, the Jesuits, and the Suplicians who carried their missions in early days of New France. An early missionary of note, Father Chrestien Le Clercq, was a Récollet priest who worked among the Micmaqs of the Gaspé Peninsula, and today ranks among the great historians of New France, through a couple of narratives he penned, "Nouvelle Relation..." and "Premier Etablissement..." The "Jesuit Relations" were letters written by missionaries to their superiors in France. The earliest documents described their first contact with Indians. (see "Récollets").

- *"Bois Brûlés"* : means "burnt woods". They were Métis people among freemen, and at a later date summer buffalo hunters of the plains competing with Indians in the Dakota Territory bison hunts. A "Brûlé" was a half-breed.

- *"Bouilli"* : fresh meat cut into small pieces and boiled, with or without spices, in voyageurs' camps.

- *"Bourgeois"* : commander of a trading fort, the highest *status*. The title "factor" was used when the "bourgeois" managed an entire region. Next in the hierarchy of the fort were the clerks in charge of the ledgers, then the traders, hunters and craftsmen. When a "bourgeois" was absent from the fort, a clerk might be temporarily appointed to assume command of the fort in his place. Clerks dressed up appropriately to share the commander's dinner table on a regular basis. The Hudson Bay company imposed a strict hierarchy in its trading forts, under two categories of employees, the officers and the servants. The "factors", bourgeois gentlemen traders, clerks and surgeons were the officers, while artisans, boatmen and laborers constituted the lower echelon category of servants.

At the bottom of the population of a fort were the "engagés", employees of fur trade companies who provided manual labor. The term was also used for canoe men, Indian or Métis men.

- *"Congés":* The early fur trade relied on independent traders and voyageurs. However, as the trade became more regulated, permits (French "congés") were issued to voyageurs.

- *"Coureur des bois":* (Wood runner) The phrase did not literally mean "runner of the woods" but described a free hunter who preferred to live in the wilderness or associated with aboriginal tribes. The first and believed to be the best of "coureurs des bois" was Etienne Brûlé who scouted for Champlain. Another who did leave a record of life among aboriginal people was Nicolas Perrot, an exceptional man and unsung hero. The woodsmen were unlicensed, unregulated, independent French traders of the 16th and 17th centuries, operating outside the regulated commerce of companies. To some, and more particularly the Catholic missionaries, such men who lived among Indians, and married into Indian groups, seemed to become "wild" ("sauvages"). A French report describes them in this fashion: 'Les Coureurs des bois, qui sans doute le mieux comprenaient leurs hôtes autochtones, étaient des illettrés et n'ont que très rarement laissé de traces écrites de leur 'ensauvagement' ("The Wood Runners who undoubtedly most understood their indigenous hosts, were uneducated and only rarely left any written traces of their own transformation into savages.") They were young adventurous men between the age of twenty and thirty-five, numbering thousands, who became assimilated to the Indian groups into which they married. Louis XIV officially terminated their way of life by signing a decree on April 15, 1676, banning all private traders and trappers from the fur trade. They gradually disappeared as the legal trade of the fur companies extended its monopoly on the western frontier.

- *"Engagés':* Indentured servants hired by farmers, merchants, entrepreneurs, missionaries and military personnel through three-year contracts, (hence nicknamed "trente-six mois" or "thirty-six months") during which time they were denied citizenship, marriage and involvement in the fur trade. They were recruited among the least favored segments of society. At the end of their contracts, they often became boatmen (canoe men), that is to say "voyageurs."

———

- *"Femmes du pays"*: Women of the fur trade, native and Métis wives, who strengthened French trade ties and alliances with native groups. They included "tent mates" and "canoe mates."

- *"Gens libres"* : Métis freemen, whose existence originated in the 18th century fur trade. The buffalo hunters of the Plains were freemen, as they worked entirely for themselves, not as employees of a company.

- *HBC - Hudson Bay Company*, London-based. For years, it was the policy of the HBC to ban marriage with Native women for their employees, in theory at least because, in practice, the top agents themselves practiced polygamy. The powerful company did not hire French Canadian voyageurs until 1815.

- *"Hiverner"* "to winter" and "Hivernants" ; winterers. The word was originally used to refer to employees of the Fur Trade who stayed in Canada during the winter. It was subsequently applied to fur trade employees who spent the winter at a trading post, and finally to refer to Métis people who spent the winter months hunting and trapping. Winter hunts of buffaloes that took place between November and March were conducted to obtain bison robes, as the buffalo hair is thick during those months. The summer hunts were to obtain meat.

- *"Hommes du Nord"*: winterers, men who spent their winters in the interior away from the posts of the St Lawrence River. These men called those who maintained their trade along the St Lawrence River, trading between Montreal and Grand Portage, "Mangeurs de lard" (bacon eaters), a pejorative name referring to their diet of salt pork.

- *"Huron"*: name given to Iroquois speaking Aboriginal people, Wendat or Wyandot, first encountered by French missionaries when they set foot in Canada. Possibly from French word "huron" meaning "ruffian." French fur traders called them "the good Iroquois."

- *"Mangeurs de lard"*: pejorative name of fat or pork eaters given to Montreal agents and voyageurs who had not yet proven themselves, novices, green horns. They were so nicknamed by the explorers of the interior because they remained around the forts along the St Lawrence River and did not venture far from them.

- *Marriage* "a la façon du pays" : (also, "a la manière du pays") literally "in the fashion of the country", or "according to local customs" followed the traditions of American Indian unions, with an exchange of gifts, no civil contract and no sanctification by any church or clergy member. Among Native groups, exchange of women was a common practice among allies. Fur traders forged close trade and kinship ties with Indians through such marriages. Often, Europeans actually had wives at home, or sometimes abandoned their fur trade mates to marry European women when they went home. However, many of those mixed marriages lasted a lifetime, and the children issued from those unions gradually began to form their own communities, the Métis communities. Intermarriages were politically and economically beneficial to both European traders and Indian groups.

- *"Mixed-blood"* : an individual also called "Métis", "bois brûlé" "brunette", "Native of Hudson Bay company," or yet "half-breed." Jacqueline Peterson, in her Ph D dissertation on French and Indian intermarriages and the Métis culture of the Great Lakes, 1680-1830, University of Illinois, 1980, calls them "The People In Between". The government of Alberta, Canada, actually made an official distinction between ethnic groups by stating that "Métis are those who fail to meet the social and legal distinctions of Native and European, but are the offspring of both." They often served as "engagés" in the French fur trade. Early Métis people had the tendency to congregate around trading posts where they would be employed as laborers and boatmen. By the end of the 19th century, companies considered the Métis to be "Indians" in their identity. In the Plains, Métis buffalo hunters operated in the trade of bison robes, and had a major role in the depletion of buffalo herds. As the bison hunts dwindled, Métis and their families resettled in other communities, often in tribal lands. Many wished to be part of treaty negotiations of 1879-1880 to claim land but had a questionable status with tribes.

- *"Mitif"* is a mixed language, primarily combining Cree and Métis French, which emerged in the 19th century. The people who gradually spoke Mitif were French and Cree speakers. Today, in the United States, there are some two hundred speakers of Mitif, most of them living in North Dakota.

- *"Nouvelle France":* a name for the French colonies of continental North America (1534-1763). New France included at first the banks of the St Lawrence River, Newfoundland and Acadia, expanding with time to include the Great Lakes Region and parts of the Appalachian region.

- *"Récollets, O.F.M. Rec"* : Friars of the St Francis Order. These Franciscans were devoted to meditation and prayer. At the same time, they were recruited to serve as military chaplains for the French army. Their order was created in the 15th century. In 1619 already, Jacques Cardon, Jacques de la Foyer and Louis Frontinier had started a mission in Acadia. When Samuel de Champlain arrived in Canada, he was accompanied by members of the Récollet Order, Father Jamet, Father Le Caron and Brother Duplessis. Another Récollet, Jean Dolbeau was assigned the territory of the Montagnais (French name for Innu aboriginal people), and the Post of Tadoussac. Joseph Le Caron was put in charge of the Huron (Wendat) mission and Denis Jamet was to oversee the missions between Quebec and Trois Rivières. The Récollet missionaries worked among indigenous peoples and recruited "truchements" (helpers) from humble backgrounds, whom they sometimes helped succeed in New France. Nicolas Marsolet, for instance, was such a recruit. Another truchement was Pierre Boucher who became governor of Trois Rivières. Gabriel Sagard was a Recollet monk who is regarded as the first religious historian of Canada and whose work commands respect. He documented those early days of the Récollet missions and details of the indigenous life they encountered in his narrative "Le Grand Voyage au Pays des Hurons." (1632). See also "Black Robes" for the work of Chrestien Le Clercq among the Micmaqs.

- *"Truchements"*: Pathfinders and scouts, intermediaries and interpreters who were cultural ambassadors.

- *«Vérandrye»* : Pierre Gautier de Varennes de la Vérandrye, also spelled «de la Verendrye». Both spellings are found in texts. "Verandrye and his band of fifty-two Frenchmen and Indians set out to reach the Mandan settlements of the Missouri" in "The Remarkable History of the Hudson Bay Company" by George Bryce, 1900, which also relates "the accounts of the daring French soldiers and explorers who disputed the claim of the Company in the 17th century."

- *"Voyageurs"* (Travelers) were half-breed boat men, canoeists for hire, skilled paddlers who facilitated travel to unknown regions by waterways during the fur trade era. It has been said that they held the first truly American profession. To best describe the life and style of these adventurers who became legendary primarily among the Canadians, I have retained the words of an unnamed retired voyageur, cited in "Les Coureurs des Bois: La Saga des Indiens Blancs", Georges-Hébert Germain (2003), a rare book which amply documents those extraordinary early days of the French presence in North America and sings of the Saga of White Indians:

"I could carry, paddle water and sing with any man I ever saw. I have been for twenty-four years a canoe man, and forty-one years in service; no portage was ever too long for me. Fifty songs could I sing. I have saved the lives of ten voyageurs, have had twelve wives and six running dogs. I spent all of my money in pleasure. Were I young again, I would spend my life the same way over. There is no life so happy as a voyageur's life."

The canoe men were young, uneducated and poor men who came primarily from France. Yet, at the end of their years of trade with various Indian tribes, and their perilous travels far away from European settlements, they became the epitome of the rugged lone American frontiersman, having survived in an incredibly difficult environment. Of such a man, Pierre Radisson, Georges-Hébert Germain writes; "At the end, he was no longer a Frenchman, or an Englishman, or an Indian, but a new combination of all these - a true inhabitant of the New World." (page 55).

Thus, in their final days, the voyageurs, fur trappers and half-breed bison hunters of the Plains who are the ancestors of today French Indians of South Dakota were among the builders of America. On page 109 of the same book, French author Germain remarked: "For the Ojibwa, Mandan, Sioux, and Hidatsa, the land would always be inhabited by the French adventurers who had built it."

ILLUSTRATIONS

www.ingramcontent.com/pod-product-compliance
Lightning Source LLC
Chambersburg PA
CBHW051445250726

48655CB00001B/246